New Tools for Changing Behavior

Alvin N. Deibert, Ph.D.   Alice J. Harmon, M.A.

Foreword by
Nathan H. Azrin, Ph.D.

Research Press Company
2612 NORTH MATTIS AVENUE • CHAMPAIGN, ILLINOIS 61820

Dr. Deibert is Psychologist for Community Health Research at Malcolm Bliss Mental Health Center, St. Louis, Missouri. Miss Harmon is a member of the staff at Tranquille School for Retarded, Tranquille, B. C., Canada. Formerly, the two authors worked as a team at the Andrew McFarland Mental Health Zone Center, Springfield, Illinois.

Foreword

The current climate of opinion has changed from the Sputnik-inspired emphasis on Science to an emphasis on Relevance. Society's desire for an increased conceptual understanding of the universe has been transformed into a desire that this understanding be translated into concrete benefits in the immediate present. In the area of learning and conditioning, animal studies in the laboratory have revealed many new facts about how behavior could be changed through the use of reinforcement. This scientific study of learning continues actively at this time.

The possible relevance of operant conditioning to practical problems of human behavior was recognized early. Books on personality, abnormal psychology, and child development began to include discussions of how specific types of human behavior problems could be analysed, interpreted and explained in terms of learning theory. This reinterpretation was then followed by actual treatment of behavior problems. Progress in this area of practical treatment has been so rapid that new journals as well as new books are appearing each year.

A desperate need at the present time is for a description of the specific details on how reinforcement principles are translated into specific procedures for a specific population. Especially great is this need for the natural practitioners of social influence; such as the parent, the physician, the hospital attendant and the teacher who are unable to devote the time necessary to learning the extensive literature on the animal studies.

The present volume is the best introduction available at this time to the non-psychologist to the specifics of practical behavior modification by reinforcement. Technical terms are avoided, and everyday concepts used in their place. Reservations that readers might have about a "mechanistic" approach and questions of propriety or ethics are often anticipated and resolved or answered. The brevity of the book makes it more likely to be read by those who desire rapid introduction, yet the specificity of the case studies provide concrete illustrations of how the procedures can be applied to mental patients, retardates, adolescents, the elderly, and children. Part 1 provides the general rationale, whereas Part 2 provides the specific application. In both Part 1 and Part 2 however, general statement and illustration are successfully combined such that the rationale and the specific procedures are never far apart.

Nathan H. Azrin

28072 17

49

iii

Contents

Instructions

The reader will find this book a little different from other books that he has read. "Question frames" have been inserted throughout the text. These "frames" are designed to give you feedback on how well you are reading the material and understanding it. They consist of a statement in which one or more blank spaces appear. You are to fill the blanks based on the material presented in the one or two paragraphs preceding it.

An identifying symbol is printed to the left of some of the frames. The symbol indicates that the answer to this frame will require you to either (1) give an original response not specifically indicated in the preceding paragraphs, or (2) recall a principle or idea presented much earlier in the book.

Answers to the question frames appear at the bottom of each page. We suggest that you take a small piece of paper or cardboard and cover the answers before formulating your responses. After you have answered the frame, slide the paper or cardboard aside and check to see if you have the correct answer. Be careful that you uncover only the answers to the frame you have just answered. There may be answers to several frames placed there and you do not want to uncover an answer to another question frame before you have had a chance to answer it. If your answer is not exactly as given but has the same meaning, you may count it as correct.

If you gave the wrong answer, review the previous one or two paragraphs. If your answer was correct, continue reading.

Be sure to write your answers in the spaces provided. Some people get lazy and just say the answer to themselves. By writing the answer, as well as thinking it, you will learn the principles and vocabulary much more quickly. You may notice that some words are used frequently as responses. This is because they are important words. The more frequently you write them the better you will remember them.

PART I

The Science of Behavior

1 The Behavioral Approach

As part of their psychology class project two boys hit upon the idea of picking out a plain, introverted shy girl on campus and "rushing" her with dates to see what effect this would have on changing her "personality." They explained the nature of the project to the other fellows in the fraternity and enlisted the participation of those who were not already pledged to other girls in dating this girl. Not only were they to date the girl but they were also instructed to be very attentive to her during the date. As the success of this project depended on the girl not finding out why she had suddenly become so popular, they were sworn to secrecy (sealed with the fraternity pledge).

A "plain Jane" was decided upon, a girl who had potential, but because of her shy and hesitant manner remained a wallflower. The "rushing" began and she soon found her weekends booked up for several weeks in advance. As the weeks passed, a change began to occur in this girl's behavior. Her appearance became animated and she began to talk and enjoy herself more on dates and with her friends. She became quite a good dancer. She changed her manner of dress and hair style. She became active in social functions outside of dating. She had now become what we usually think of as "extroverted" as opposed to her previous "introverted" manner.

1. A change in this girl's _____

occurred as a result of her being dated by frater-

nity boys.

The change was so remarkable that even after the project was completed, some of the fraternity boys continued to date her. She even began to receive requests for dates from fellows from other fraternities.

---

1. behavior

It would not be difficult for us to agree that this girl underwent a striking change in "personality." From a withdrawn, socially shy girl, she became a social butterfly. The frequency of her social activity increased. Her dress and hair styling changed. Her facial expression changed. She underwent other changes in her behavior. As a result, we say that she underwent a "personality" change.

2. Because we observed a change in this girl's

_____ we say she underwent

a "personality" change.

It would be interesting to imagine what would have happened to this girl if she had gone to the college counseling services with the complaint that she didn't get any dates from boys, felt shy around people, and lacked confidence. One can guess that it would have involved one or two sessions a week in therapy (group or individual). She would most likely have been required to explore her relationship with her parents. Attempts would be made to help her understand feelings that relate to her attitude. Advice on how to make herself more attractive to others would be expected. Of course, there is no assurance that this would have resulted in her getting more dates. Another approach (depending on the therapist) may have simply been to help this girl accept her unpopularity and learn to live with and by herself.

We see, though, that because of an increase in the frequency of one behavior—dating boys—many other behaviors also changed for the better. The problem didn't appear to arise from something within the girl herself. It was, rather, the result of a social condition over which she had little, if any, control. Once this problem was corrected, many other behavioral difficulties cleared up also.

A New Understanding of "Personality"

A new understanding of "personality" is developing based on the discovery that our behavior is more the result of external social or behavioral forces operating on us (as was the case of our wallflower above) rather than to "things" going on inside of us.

3. "Personality" results from the influence of external

_____ or _____

forces acting upon us.

---

2. behavior   3. social, behavioral

"Personality" Is the Behavior a Person Performs

What we really refer to when we speak of "personality" are the behaviors we see a person performing. We don't see a "personality"; we merely observe a person's behaviors. In the case of our college wallflower, we did not see "introvert" stamped on her anywhere. We couldn't cut her brain open and find a lump of introversion. We did, however, observe her behavior (how frequently she dated boys, how frequently she engaged in social activities, how frequently she talked with people, how frequently she smiled, etc.) and then lumped all these behaviors together under the label of "introvert."

> 4. When we speak of "personality" we are really
>
> referring to ——————————— we see a
>
> person performing.

Thus, this new understanding directs our attention to the *behavior* of the individual. It indicates that we need to change or modify *behaviors* that the individual (or concerned others) feel are preventing him from attaining maximum adjustment.

> 5. The new approach in psychology refers to changes
>
> in ——————————— not in "personality."

The Error of "Labeling" People

"Labeling" persons (such as "introvert") is no longer an acceptable approach for understanding adjustment problems because labels do not permit us to identify the specific behavioral difficulties that are interfering with the person's adjustment. Labeling an individual as an "introvert" does not tell us which specific behaviors this individual does or does not engage in that make us feel he is an "introvert." If we don't know what these specific behaviors are then we don't know in what ways his behavior patterns have to be changed to make him "not-introverted."

---

4. behavior

5. behavior

6. We no longer _____ people
   with adjustment problems because we need to
   know the specific _____ peo-
   ple are performing before we can change them.

Labels for adjustment problems or "personality" problems are also misleading in another way. They imply that the individual is this way under all conditions and at all times. We are aware, however, that this is not an accurate picture of how people behave. Our behavior frequently changes with the situation. Some individuals talk little around strangers, but are very talkative among their close friends. On the other hand, I have heard a mother say, "I couldn't believe that was my son. He's never that talkative around the house." Behavior is generally relative to a particular situation. Only by studying the relationship between an individual's behavioral responses and the situations or conditions under which they occur can we discover ways to change the behavior so as to increase one's adjustment to and satisfaction from life in general.

7. Only by observing the relationship between
   _____ and the conditions
   under which it occurs can we discover ways to
   _____ it.

Behavior Changes Result in Attitude Changes

Finally, this new understanding teaches us that "as our behaviors go, so go our feelings or emotions." If our behavior is what we want it to be and desired results or goals are being achieved, then the feelings of satisfaction, happiness, enjoyment, etc., follow. If our behavior is not what we want it to be and desired results are not obtained, we feel frustrated, disappointed, unhappy, angry, upset, etc. Our wallflower didn't have to become "happy" and "socially confident" before becoming involved in social affairs and dating. She first had to have dates and become involved in social affairs and then the feelings of social confidence and happiness followed. That is to say, many times behavior change comes before emotional change, not the reverse.

---

6. label,   7. behavior
   behaviors   change

8. We frequently need to make a _____

change before we can expect a change in our

_____.

Talking Versus Behaving

Our earlier approach to adjustment problems involved what we have all come to know as "analysis" or "therapy." The individual spends many weeks or months talking out his problem. The idea was that in talking about his past history and present problem the patient would eventually come to understand the reasons for his difficulties, and then learn to live with the problem or overcome it. Emphasis was placed on obtaining insight into the problem. The feeling was that your behavior would correct itself as you came to understand it.

9. The earlier approach to adjustment problems required the individual to spend long periods of time _____ out his difficulties.

The new approach asserts that such analysis is not absolutely necessary for behavioral correction or change. It attacks the problem directly by attempting to determine and change the external social or behavioral conditions which are causing the behavior. If the external social or behavioral forces acting on the individual to cause his behavior can be changed, then his own behavior will change accordingly. One rearranges the external conditions and the individual's behavior also rearranges itself. Dealing directly with changes in external conditions is a short cut method of accomplishing the same thing that the earlier "talking" approaches attempted to accomplish.

10. If external social or behavioral forces acting on a person are _____ his behavior will _____.

An individual may not be behaving appropriately by his own or a concerned loved one's standards. Both the old and new approaches attempt to help the individual to change in such a way so the person himself and/or concerned loved ones in his life are no longer distressed. The earlier approach would require the individual to undergo extensive self-examination in order to understand why he is behaving in a distressed

---

8. behavior
feeling (emotions)

9. talking

10. changed
change

8 or inappropriate manner. The new approach would be to set up a program to directly change the external environment of the person thereby bringing about a change in his behavior. The long time spent in talking out one's problem required by the earlier approach is avoided.

> 11. A new approach to treating behavior problems
>
> is to _____ the relationship be-
>
> tween a person and his _____
>
> environment.

This new approach maintains that inappropriate and distressing behaviors (as well as "normal" behaviors) occur mainly because social or behavioral forces external to the person (mainly involving parents, spouse, peers, etc.) in some way encourage and *support* the behavior. Treatment requires one to discover what these "supports" are. They must then be removed or modified.

> 12. Inappropriate behavior occurs because social or
>
> behavioral forces involving parents, spouse, etc.
>
> _____ it. Treatment requires
>
> that these _____ be removed
>
> or modified.

Scientific Foundations of a Behavioral Approach

Perhaps the most important part of this new treatment approach for changing behavior is that it is based on sound scientific principles. This is the first time that a treatment system for human problems has been based on experimentally obtained information rather than on personal speculation or opinion. Principles have been discovered in the laboratory setting under strict experimental controls. In fact, some of these principles are so basic that they have taken on the status of a law. Just as there are laws governing the physical world (gravitation,

---

11. change
    external

12. support
    supports

gas laws, motion laws, etc.) so there are laws governing the behavioral world of living organisms, including humans. These laws have been shown to have a strong influence over a broad range of behaviors from the simplest organisms to complex humans.

13. Just as there are laws for the physical world there

are also laws for the _____

world of living organisms.

Much of the research in the area of behavioral laws began in the study of animal behavior in the laboratory. Pigeons, white rats, dogs and monkeys are the most popular subjects. This is in general their ranking in order of the complexity of their behavior. The pigeon has the simplest behavioral responses, the white rat is next, the dog third, and the monkey has the most complex.

14. _____ _____

were first discovered in the animal laboratory.

In the laboratory, it has been shown that the same laws that determine the pigeon's behavior also determines the monkey's. It may be more difficult to see the law operating in the monkey because his behaviors are more complex, but with careful study, the law's effects are soon evident.

15. Behavior laws operate in _____
    animals.

From the monkey the next step is the human being. Although it is a giant step between the monkey and the human the same basic laws are still operating. As complex as human behavior appears, it still follows some basic laws. One must admit that there are probably many more laws to be discovered, but the few we already know about explain a lot of our behavior.

16. As complex as human behavior appears, it still

    follows _____ _____.

---

13. behavioral   15. all

14. behavioral laws   16. basic laws

10   The new approach in psychology is the use of these laws in treating and changing human behavior in such a way as to make persons better satisfied with themselves and/or more adjusted or adapted to their social environment.

That these approaches are impressively successful is attested to by an ever-growing body of data from their clinical application. Professional publications in the field of psychology carry examples of this kind of work and its application to nearly every kind of human problem. The fact that this new emphasis is able to effect such impressive "readjustments" after a prolonged history of non-adjustment, holds out great promise that it may prove to be of even greater benefit in preventive approaches to mental illness.

17. The hope of this new approach to behavioral problems is that it will be effective in

_____ such problems from developing.

Purposes of This Manual

The purposes of this manual are two-fold: (1) to present the basic principles of this new science of behavior and (2) show how they can be used to handle day-to-day problems in living that develop in our relationship with others. The hope is that in this manner many living problems that would normally arise as a result of inappropriate interactions between individuals (especially parents and children) can be prevented before they get out of hand and develop into more serious problems.

18. By knowing the principles of behavior we can

_____ problems in living from developing or getting out of hand.

---

17. preventing

18 prevent

This manual is divided into two major parts. The first part (Chapters 2, 3, and 4) will introduce you to the basic laws or principles which have been discovered by behavioral scientists. It is, therefore, a basic course in the science of behavior.

19. This manual is to be a basic course in the

_____.

Because animal studies contributed so much to our discovery of behavioral laws, we will introduce each new law in Chapter 3 with an example of how this law was first studied in the animal lab. We will then show how this same principle is operating to affect human behaviors.

Part II (Chapters 5, 6, 7, and 8) shows how these basic laws are being applied in the treatment of children with behavioral problems, in training the retarded child in acquiring the basic skills in living, and applications to adolescent and adult problems in living. Aldous Huxley once said, "pure science does not remain pure indefinitely. Sooner or later it is apt to turn into applied science and finally into technology." Part II is the applied part of the basic principles presented in Chapters 2 and 3.

20. Part I is pure science; Part II is _____

_____.

_____

19. science of behavior

20. applied science

2 The Basic Law

The behavioral scientist believes that our behavior is influenced by principles or laws. He studies the behavior of animals and humans in order to uncover these laws. Behavioral laws operate throughout our lives to determine our responses in various situations. Whether a child responds to his parents' refusal to grant his wishes with a shrug of the shoulder or a temper tantrum depends on behavioral laws operating in similar encounters in the past. How a parent responds to a child's demands likewise depends on behavioral laws operating in the situation based on previous encounters with the child. In most cases, we are not aware of their operation. Nevertheless their influence affects our present and future behavior.

By uncovering the laws influencing our behavior the scientist hopes to be able to use this information to change or modify behavior when necessary. By knowing and understanding how such laws operate to effect our behavior we can use them in helping us to prevent or eliminate some of the human problems that are present in the world. If we are aware of how behavioral laws operate, we can hopefully use these laws to improve our lives and the lives of those with whom we associate. Where individuals are already in "distress" we can apply the law in an appropriate manner in order to "correct" the situation.

1. By understanding how the laws of behavior oper-

   ate we can use them to help us _____

   or _____ human problems.

Common Sense Versus Science

Most of us unknowingly admit to some simple belief in the idea that there are laws effecting our behavior. This is indicated by our use of such sayings as "spare the rod and spoil the child," "children are to

---

1. prevent
   eliminate

be seen and not heard," "monkey see, monkey do," etc. Such sayings arose however, out of folk-lore and are not the outcome of sound scientific investigations. They are also not very clearly stated and are therefore difficult to use in actual practice. Some also appear to be incorrect in light of sound scientific evidence.

2. Many of our ideas about raising children arise

from _____ rather than sound

_____ investigations.

In the past few years behavioral scientists have been studying some elementary laws of behavior discovered in the laboratory under strict experimental controls. Once having been discovered, these laws are studied under conditions other than the one in which they were originally uncovered. Their effects are then observed under these new and varied settings to see if they continue to have a strong influence over behavior. This is the way a new drug is tested before being released for human use. It is first given to lower animals for thorough screening and then used on humans under strict controls before being put on the market. The laws of behavior to be studied in this manual have undergone similarly rigorous tests. They are now being used to bring about behavioral changes in people, often with dramatic results.

3. The now known behavioral laws have been

studied in the _____ under

strict experimental controls.

As our understanding of the conditions under which these principles are effective increases and we learn to apply them with more precision, behavioral changes will be brought about even more efficiently and quickly. What will be the outcome of increased precision in their use remains to be seen, but the possibilities for individual development and self-fulfillment are indeed exciting.

4. As our understanding of behavioral laws increases

our use of them for behavioral _____

will become more _____.

_____

2. folklore   3. laboratory   4. change
   scientific   precise (effective)

A basic law of behavior discovered by the behavioral scientist in the laboratory is known as the "law of reinforcement." This basic law states that living organisms tend to repeat those behaviors that result in rewards (desirable outcomes) and tend to avoid those behaviors that fail to produce rewards. To state it another way, the "law of reinforcement" says: (1) Any behavior that is followed by a rewarding (desirable) outcome is likely to be repeated. The behavior is likely to *increase in frequency*. (2) Any behavior that is not followed by a reward will tend not to be repeated. The behavior is likely to *decrease in frequency*.

5. The law of reinforcement states that all living

   organisms tend to repeat behaviors that lead to

   _____ and tend to _____

   behaviors that do not produce a reward.

To be consistent with the law of reinforcement we therefore have to assume that any behavior which is repeated again and again must be producing a reward (desired outcome). Otherwise, according to the law of reinforcement it would not reoccur. Only behaviors that produce rewards (desired outcomes) tend to be repeated. Therefore, if we observe a behavior occurring repeatedly we have to assume that there is present in the situation some reward or desired outcome which supports it.

6. _____ is the central principle

   of behavior training.

Here lies the clue to our new approach to behavioral change: *The realization that any behavior which an individual performs over and over again is being supported by a reward (desired outcome).*

7. Behaviors which are repeated are _____

   _____.

---

5. rewards   6. reward
   avoid (not repeat)   7. supported by a reward

Therefore, if a desired or appropriate behavioral response is not learned we must assume that efforts in that direction have not provided the individual an appropriate reward for the behavior. Teaching new behaviors or increasing the frequency of occurrence of desirable or appropriate behaviors depends upon our supplying appropriate rewards to the individual whenever he performs the behavior.

8. If an individual is not performing a behavior we

   want him to, it is quite likely he is not getting

   _____ for it.

Even more revolutionary however is the realization that inappropriate or undesirable behaviors which occur are also being supported by a reward. No matter how distressing the outcome of an inappropriate response may appear on first observation, there must be a reward occurring in the situation that is causing the individual to repeat the behavior. Indeed, the reward must be so important that the behavior continues in spite of the unpleasant results that follow it. The unique contribution of the behavioral scientist is in directing our attention toward discovering the *rewards* that support such inappropriate responses and removing them. The behavior should accordingly disappear.

9. Inappropriate or undesirable behaviors persist

   because they are _____.

Other Conditions To Be Considered

The law of reinforcement as stated (p. 15) seems quite definite in how one would bring about behavioral change. It would seem that all we have to do in order to get individuals to behave in an appropriate manner is to (1) reward those behaviors we want the person to perform and (2) withhold the reward from those behaviors we wish to see stopped. Basically, one would be correct. In real life, however, situations are not so simple to arrange. There are other conditions that make this basic approach more difficult to achieve than it would at first appear. The law of reinforcement doesn't operate in such a simple way because there are environmental situations and other behavioral principles that influence its effect.

---

8. rewarded
9. rewarded

10. If you desire to see a behavior increase in frequency _____ it. If you desire to see a behavior decrease in frequency

_____.

This is the case with any basic law. Galileo, for example, stated that objects, regardless of their weight, size or shape fall at the same speed. If objects are dropped from the same height they should reach the earth at the same time. We know, however, that most of the time this doesn't happen. We know that if we drop a feather and a rock from the same height at the same time, the rock reaches the ground before the feather. The fact of the matter is that Galileo's observation applies only to the ideal situation where there is a perfect vacuum. In the "real" world, however, there is no such thing as a perfect vacuum. Thus, this law does not hold up in the "real" world because there are other conditions to be considered which affect the operation of this law. Such conditions as air currents and the feather's weight and shape cause it to be influenced more by the wind, hence it drops to the earth more slowly.

In the same way, conditions present in the "real" world influence the operation of the law of reinforcement. These conditions tend to disguise the fact that this basic law is operating to determine our behavior.

11. Environmental situations and other behavioral principles tend to _____ the fact that the law of reinforcement is operating in our lives to determine our _____.

Determining the Rewards

The most important thing we need to do in order to make use of the law of reinforcement in improving the behavior of others and ourselves is to find out those things people find rewarding. Until we know this, we cannot supply the appropriate reward for the appropriate behavior we wish to see the person performing. In the same manner, until we know what the reward is that is supporting an inappropriate

---

10. reward
    withhold the reward

11. disguise
    behavior

18   response we will not be able to remove it. By knowing the rewards people seek we can be sure that the behaviors we want to occur can be rewarded and behavior we don't want to occur will go unrewarded.

12. The most important thing we need to do to

_____ behavior is find out

the _____ which is support-

ing it.

Most people find money a very powerful reward. It is easy to find situations where people are performing particular behaviors in order to receive money. One could also indicate situations where a particular behavior would stop if the money were withheld. The reason for money being such a powerful reward for behavior is that it can be used to obtain many other kinds of specific rewards such as food, clothing, travel, medical care, stature, power, etc.

School children who understand their school subjects and get a lot of correct answers on tests (which is very rewarding) will tend to have greater interest in school and study more than students who fail to understand their subjects and get few correct answers on tests (very non-rewarding). Students who continue to get few correct answers on tests in most or all of their studies many times *decrease* the frequency of school attendance and may even drop out of school completely to avoid spending every day in a non-rewarding situation.

Many teenage boys go through a period when the family car becomes a very desirable reward. Use of the car can be used by the parents as a reward for appropriate behavior. One could go on and list any number of things that people find rewarding and for which they would make an appropriate response to obtain.

13. We can assume that a _____

is operating to maintain any behavior which

occurs.

Attention Is Rewarding

One of the most important discoveries made by the behavioral scientist was that *attention* is a very powerful reward, especially for

---

12. change
    reward

13. reward

children. Research is beginning to demonstrate that people do many
things merely for the attention it brings them. Consider for a moment what it would be like if no one paid any attention to you. How would you feel if people walked away from you when you started to speak to them? What if, when you started to speak in a group of people, you were interrupted and the other people continued to talk as if you did not exist. The thought of such behavior on the part of other people is truly frightening to most of us.

14. _____ is a powerful reward

for most people, especially children.

Attention may or may not be given in the form of praise or approval. Attention by itself can be very rewarding. But if, when we are attending to a person, we also give some indication of approval or praise, it becomes even more rewarding. Because approval, praise or attention (showing interest in a person by observing what he is doing) is satisfying to the individual, we can use this as a reward to encourage the kind of behaviors we want him to perform or learn. If a person does something we would like to see him do again, we should call attention to this behavior by approving or praising it.

15. When a person performs a low frequency be-

havior we want to increase, we should _____

him with _____.

Following are some examples of how approval or praise can be used to reward a behavior and thus increase the likelihood that it will be repeated.

(1) Betty Jane helped her mother with the dishes after dinner. When they had finished, the mother squeezed Betty Jane in her arms and told her how lucky she was to have such an efficient dish drier.

(2) Mr. Frank came home from work one evening to find that his wife had prepared a special candlelight dinner. After dinner he kissed his wife and told her how much he enjoyed a meal served under such a romantic atmosphere.

(3) Tommy came in from playing outside. It was one of those rare times when he stopped to wipe his shoes on the mat. His mother thanked him for being so considerate of her floor.

---

14. attention

15. reward
    attention (praise) (approval)

(4) Sally, who generally doesn't eat any carrots, made an attempt to eat some during dinner. Her mother complimented her on her adventurous spirit.

(5) Ted had been sitting alone in his room for about an hour doing his homework. His father came in with a cup of hot chocolate for him and told him he thought he'd enjoy the break after studying for so long.

16. In these examples the attention and praise given for these behaviors served as a ———————.

17. As a result, the frequency of these behaviors is likely to ————————————.

Failing To Attend

The law of reinforcement also tells us that a behavior can be reduced in frequency or made *not* to occur by withholding a reward. We have just seen how attention paired with praise can be a powerful reward to get people to repeat behaviors we want to see performed. It would then seem that withholding attention and praise from a behavior would result in its not occurring again.

18. The law of reinforcement tells us that behaviors

can be ——————————————

by withholding ——————————.

We have all, at some time, heard a person remark, "If so-and-so doesn't appreciate what I'm doing, I'll stop doing it." What is usually meant is that somebody important to us isn't paying attention to what we are doing.

19. Behaviors that are not ——————————

with ——————————— are likely not to be

repeated again.

---

16. reward

17. increase

18. reduced in frequency (made not to occur)
    attention (praise) (approval)

19. rewarded
    attention (praise) (approval)

People (especially children) need to receive attention (especially in the form of praise). Withholding attention can be distressing. If we ignore a particular behavior the person will be less likely to repeat it.

(1) If Tommy wiped his shoes on the mat and mother showed no sign of paying attention, Tommy would probably not think of wiping his shoes the next time.

(2) If Mr. Frank said nothing to his wife after the candlelight dinner, the chances are that Mrs. Frank would think her husband is not interested in such things and would likely not repeat it.

(3) If Sally makes an attempt to eat her carrots and her parents do not call attention to her adventurous spirit, she may not make another attempt.

20. Because these behaviors were not rewarded with

_____ they most probably

will _____.

Attention Supports Inappropriate Behavior

If attention works to increase or decrease appropriate behaviors, it exerts the same influence on inappropriate responses. They too can be increased or decreased depending upon whether or not they are rewarded with attention.

21. Just as attention increases the frequency of ap-

propriate behaviors it also _____

the frequency of inappropriate behaviors.

It has been in their failure to understand this effect that people (especially parents) have found it very difficult to bring many inappropriate responses under control. For example, it's quite natural for many parents to use punishment (spanking, verbal threats, etc.) to attempt to control their children and stop inappropriate responses on their part. In the light of our previous discussion we can see why they often fail in spite of such efforts to stop it. There simply cannot be a

---

20. attention (praise) (approval)
   not be repeated

21. increases

"pure" case of punishment because everytime a parent punishes a child he is *at the same time rewarding* the child with *attention*. For some children, the reward of attention is more important than the accompanying punishment and they persist in their inappropriate behavior merely for the attention it provides. A more complete discussion of this problem and its implications is treated in Chapter 5.

22. Punishment is many times ineffective in eliminating inappropriate behavior because the person is at the same time _____ with _____.

23. A better way to reduce the frequency of inappropriate behavior is to _____ from it.

Even the well-meaning approach toward behavioral difficulties may result in strengthening inappropriate rather than appropriate responses. The well intended sympathy and attention given to persons suffering from physical incapacities may actually serve to increase their physical handicaps rather than reduce them. This problem as it relates to mental retardation is discussed in Chapter 6. There is even evidence to indicate that some of our behavioral approaches toward the elderly actually serve to increase their behavioral deterioration (see Chapter 8). Research is also demonstrating how our behaviors toward the mentally ill actually serve to "lock" them in their illness rather than rehabilitate them for normal behavioral responses (see Chapter 8).

So it is that research into behavioral laws not only points out the value of attention in encouraging appropriate behaviors but the equal importance of withholding attention from, or ignoring, inappropriate behaviors in order to eliminate them.

---

22. rewarded
   attention

23. withhold attention

3 Subprinciples

As indicated in the previous chapter we need to be aware of some other principles in addition to the basic "law of reinforcement" in order to understand how our behaviors are learned or unlearned. Like the "law of reinforcement" itself, these conditions have been studied in the laboratory. Investigation of these principles under scientifically controlled situations shows their influence on the "law of reinforcement" to be very predictable. We will discuss these principles under the headings of: **Timing; Pairing; Scheduling;** and **Shaping.**

1. In addition to the basic _____ _____ there are several other principles we need to know in order to understand our _____.

2. The four principles we will study here are: _____; _____ _____; and _____.

Timing

The principle of Timing has a very important influence on the law of reinforcement. It tells us when we have to apply rewards in order for them to be effective. If we want to get the greatest benefit from the use of rewards, we have to know when to use them. In this way the connection between the behavior we want performed and the reward for performing it is easily learned.

3. The principle of Timing is concerned with the _____ between a behavior and a reward.

---

1. law of reinforcement
   behavior

2. timing   scheduling
   pairing   shaping

3. connection

Research in both animal and human learning has shown that for rewards to have their greatest effect, they should come *immediately* after the behavior occurs. Animals and humans learn better if the results of their behavior occur *immediately*. The longer the reward is withheld the more difficult it is for the individual to connect the behavior with the reward. The longer it takes to make this connection, the longer it takes for appropriate behavior to be learned.

4. Rewards that occur _____ after a behavior result in better learning.

If the reward does not follow immediately after a behavior a child will continue to make other responses. The response that happens to occur just before the reward will be the one connected with the reward. A child will tend to repeat that response rather than the one we want him to repeat. This is the response that will be learned very quickly.

5. A child connects a _____ with the response that comes immediately _____ it.

6. Children do not learn as well if the reward is _____ rather than given _____.

How This Principle Is Used in Teaching School Subjects

Knowing whether or not he is making correct responses to arithmetic or spelling problems is very rewarding to a child. As long as he *knows* that he is making correct responses he will continue to perform. When he starts to make a number of mistakes he quickly gives up. This indicates that success in learning is a powerful reward. It also demonstrates that children learn school subjects much better if they are told immediately how well they are doing.

---

4. immediately

5. reward
   before

6. delayed
   immediately

7. Children learn school subjects best if they are
given _____ knowledge of how
they are doing.

Because of this, people interested in education have developed a device called a "teaching machine." These machines present the child with a small bit of information, ask him a question about it to see if he has understood it, and then *immediately* tell him if he is correct or not. (Usually a little window pops open exposing the correct answer which he then compares with the answer he gave.) This is quite different from the old-fashioned way of drilling children on a lesson for days or weeks and giving them a test at the end of it all. Using such machines, 3- and 4-year-old children learn school subjects which only first and second graders can learn under the old-fashioned way. In one pre-school, the children enjoyed their lessons so much that they liked to spend their recess "playing" with their teaching machines rather than play outside in the sand box.

8. The important principle to remember is this:
For rewards to be most effective they must be
given _____ after the behavior
occurs that we want the children to learn.

Pairing

The last example given on page 20 of the previous chapter was of a father bringing a cup of hot chocolate to his son after he had been busily studying in his room for about an hour. This example was used to show how attention from the father might reward studying and encourage his son in this behavior. There is another reward present in this situation. That is the hot chocolate. There are actually two rewards present—hot chocolate and attention.

---

7. immediate

8. immediately

If attention or praise is rewarding by itself, then *pairing* this with a physical reward will make the pay-off even more rewarding. There is, then, an even greater likelihood that the behavior will be repeated. Putting two types of reward together at the same time makes it even more certain that the person will want to repeat the behavior which produces them.

9. Attention ———————————— with a physical

   reward increases the likelihood that a behavior

   will be repeated.

There is another reason why attention or praise should be paired with a physical reward. For some children praise or attention may not be as desirable as a physical pay-off. Very young children and severely retarded children respond to candy, food, and toys more than to an adult's praise or attention. This is probably because they don't understand the words but they do appreciate sweets, toys, etc. For young children it is useful to pair the two rewards. The pleasure of the physical reward is then connected with the attention or praise. Soon the attention or praise will have as much or more value than the physical reward.

10. Very young children tend to respond more to

    ———————————————————— than to

    ————————————————————.

11. It is best to ———————————— attention

    with a physical reward to begin training.

An Animal Study Illustrating the Principle of "Pairing"

In the laboratory one group of rats was given training in pressing a bar for a small bit of food. They learned this very quickly. The experimenter then turned off the food delivery mechanism and the rats received no more food for pressing the bar. This group of rats soon gave up pressing the bar. At the same time another group of rats was trained to press a bar for food but just before the bit of food arrived a buzzer sounded. In this group, the experimenter turned off the food delivery mechanism so that the bar-press no longer produced food but it continued to produce the sound of the buzzer. This group of rats

---

continued to press the bar for a much longer time than the other group. 27
We see that the value of the food reward became connected with the buzzer. The rats continued to press the bar for a long time simply for the reward of hearing the buzzer.

12. In this study the food was _____ with a buzzer.

13. The rats who received the buzzer but no food pressed the bar _____ than the rats who received neither food nor buzzer.

14. This indicates that the buzzer having been paired with the food, had now become a
_____.

Examples of How "Pairing" Can Be Used in Everyday Situations

In the same way, the pairing of approval or praise with a physical reward (candy, toy, etc.) makes verbal rewards more desirable to children. Their influence over behavior persists long after the physical rewards are no longer given. Nature uses this principle in strengthening the mother-child relationship by requiring the infant to depend upon the mother's body for its nourishment. Taking milk (physical reward) from the mother becomes connected with the mother's presence and attention. Soon the infant desires merely the presence of the mother.

15. Praising a child and giving him a gold star at the same time illustrates the principle of
_____.

16. A mother is teaching her child to use the toilet. She hugs him and gives him a piece of candy after a bowel-movement on the toilet. Soon the child will seek only the _____ as the reward.

---

12. paired   13. longer   14. reward   15. pairing   16. hug

28   Tommy's mother could have made more certain he would have wiped his shoes on the mat the next time if she had paired her praise of him with a cookie. If Mr. Frank wanted to really be sure his wife served dinner by candlelight more frequently, he could have made an effort to bring his wife some flowers the following evening and again complimented her on the previous evening's dinner. (This probably wouldn't be necessary, however, since compliments from husbands for dinner are so rare that flowers add very little to the value of the praise!)

17. A child could be taught to put his toys away after he is done playing by calling attention to his neatness and, at the same time, giving him a ——————————— of juice or candy.

Scheduling

The principle of scheduling rewards has to do with how frequently they are given. The timing principle and the scheduling principle should not be confused. The *timing* principle covers the *speed* with which a reward is given. The *scheduling* principle indicates how *frequently* a reward is given. This principle can be broken down into two phases, the phase of *continuous scheduling* and the phase of *partial scheduling*.

18. The ——————————— principle relates to the immediacy with which a reward is given.

19. The scheduling principle indicates how ——————————— a reward is given.

Continuous Scheduling

When a child is first learning a behavior it is very important that he be given as much information as possible. In this way he learns very quickly and easily what behaviors are correct or acceptable and which ones are incorrect, or unacceptable. To put it another way, the

---

17. physical reward

18. timing

19. frequently (often)

more rewards a child gets the sooner he "catches on" to what is expected of him. He learns very quickly that "if I do such and such, I
get a reward." If he desires the reward he'll soon be doing what you
require or expect of him.

In the first stages of learning new behaviors, it is important for
the child to be rewarded every time he performs the behavior. This
is what one means by *continuous scheduling*. The behavior is followed
by a reward every time (100% of the time).

> 20. Continuous scheduling indicates that in the
>
>   initial stages of learning it is important for a
>
>   child to get a reward _____
>
>   he performs the behavior.

Partial Scheduling

Once the child has learned a behavior and is doing it as well as
he can, it is then possible to change to a *partial schedule*. This means
that the frequency of the rewards can be decreased. This will not,
however, decrease the frequency of the behavior. Once a behavior is
learned it will continue at the same frequency even though rewards
are not given every time.

> 21. Decreasing the frequency of rewards after a child
>
>   has learned a response _____
>
>   decrease the frequency of the behavior.

The principle of *partial scheduling* is very useful. Because of this
principle parents can keep behavior going without having to spend a
lot of time giving rewards. If parents had to reward desired behavior
every time it occurred in order to keep it going this would be very
impractical and child-raising would be a most difficult task.

> 22. Once a child has learned a response we can
>
>   _____ by making use
>
>   of the principle of _____.

---

20. every time (whenever)   22. keep it going
21. will not   partial scheduling

A pigeon was taught to peck at a small hole whenever a green light turned on. If the pigeon pecked at the hole when the green light came on, a small grain of corn fell out onto the floor in front of the panel on which the light was mounted. When the pigeon was first being taught this "trick," a grain of corn fell out *every* time he pecked at the hole when the green light was on. If the light was not on, nothing happened when he pecked at the hole. He quickly learned to connect pecking when the green light was on with the grain of corn. He soon gave up pecking at the hole whenever it was off.

After the pigeon learned to peck continually in the presence of the light the pay-offs were reduced. He no longer got a grain of corn every time he pecked in the presence of the green light. At first he received a grain of corn for every other peck (50% of the time) and then it was reduced to every fourth peck (25% of the time) and eventually he was receiving a grain of corn once in every 100 pecks. Amazingly enough, the pigeon continued to peck away in the presence of the green light even faster than he did at the beginning. The pigeon had been slowly weaned from expecting a reward for every peck. As a result, the frequency with which he responded was not lessened.

23. The pigeon in this example was weaned from a

_____ schedule of pay-offs to a

_____ schedule.

Another interesting situation also develops as a result of our weaning the pigeon to a *partial schedule* of pay-offs. If we stop rewarding the pigeon completely (not one single grain of corn ever again) he will continue to peck away in the presence of the green light *longer* than if he had been rewarded continuously (100% of the time). If the pigeon received a grain of corn for every peck in the presence of the green light and we suddenly stop giving the corn, the pigeon would quickly give up. If however, he has been receiving a grain of corn only after 100 or 200 pecks he will continue to peck for a long time before he "catches on" to the fact that no more corn is being given as a reward for a peck. He may peck several thousand times before he stops completely. *Partial* scheduling not only keeps a behavior occurring at a high frequency, it also prolongs the length of time before the animal stops responding once the response no longer produces the reward.

---

23. continuous
    partial

24. Partial scheduling prolongs the time before the individual _____ responding once the response no longer produces the

_____ .

How "Partial Scheduling" Serves To Maintain Behavior

The same principle works with children. Once they have learned behavior it can be maintained by rewarding the child only once in a while. At first we reward the child every time he performs the behavior. After he has learned to perform the behavior very well, we need only reward him some of the time. We slowly reduce the frequency of our rewards but the behavior continues to occur at a high frequency.

25. When first training children we should reward them _____ they respond correctly. After they have learned a response, we need only reward them _____ of the time.

The importance of a *gradual reduction* in the frequency of giving a reward *only after* a behavior is well established cannot be stressed too much. You will notice that this warning has two parts to it. (1) The behavior must be well-established, and (2) the reduction in the pay-off must be gradual. If you reduce the pay-offs before the response is thoroughly learned you will slow its progress. If you reduce the pay-offs too *quickly* after the response is learned you may cause it to drop off. There are not any strict guidelines that can be given to decide if a response is well learned or not. That will have to be left up to your own judgment based on what your expectation for the child is and his capabilities.

26. Rewards must be reduced very _____ after a response is learned or it may decrease in frequency (drop off).

---

24. stops
    reward

25. every time
    part (some)

26. gradually (slowly)

32

27. A parent need compliment a child on superior study habits at home only very _____ (ly) to maintain them at a high frequency, provided the behavior has become well-established through a schedule of rewards and these were reduced very _____.

Guidelines for "Partial Scheduling"

A rough guideline can be given, however, for the gradual reduction in the use of rewards. When one decides to shift over from a continuous schedule to a partial schedule it is usually safe to drop down to an 80% pay-off schedule (administer rewards approximately 4 times out of 5) and then a 50% schedule (approximately every other time) and then a 30% schedule and eventually one need reward only once in a great while. Again, one is cautioned that these are not hard and fast rules. When it is indicated that the child should be rewarded "approximately 4 out of 5 times" this does not mean that you have to keep a precise count of when you reward him and skip the fifth time. It merely indicates that when you first shift to a partial pay-off schedule you still continue to "reward" more than you "fail to reward." Similarly, when you drop to a 50% pay-off schedule the important thing to remember is to "reward" about as often as you "fail to reward." One should not follow a strict schedule of "every other time."

28. In shifting from a continuous schedule to a partial schedule one can follow the rough guidelines of reducing the pay-off schedule to _____% of the time, _____% of the time, _____% of the time and finally once in a great while.

The principle of partial scheduling and its effect on behavior operates to maintain some of the undesirable or inappropriate behaviors of children that seem to resist our attempts to stop them. This simply

---

27. rarely (infrequently)
    gradually (slowly)

28. 80
    50
    30

results from the lack of awareness on our part that we have the child
on a partial pay-off schedule. The behavior pays off part of the time
and as a result persists despite our best (or worst) efforts to get it
stopped.

29. Many undesirable behaviors persist in children

because we have them on a _____

pay-off schedule and don't realize it.

An Example of How "Partial Scheduling" Maintains Inappropriate Behavior

For example, a child is normally not permitted to watch a program
on TV past 8 o'clock. One evening the child wants to stay up later and
watch TV. The parents initially refuse. He continues to pester them
and thinks up excuses and reasons for being permitted to watch TV
past the appointed hour. As this is interfering with their enjoyment of
the program, they give in and let him stay up a half-hour longer. Parents
usually find themselves saying, "But just for tonight." A few evenings
later he tries it again, but this time they insist he go to bed. Eventually
he tries it again a few nights later and after some pestering and making
excuses, etc. they give in and let him stay up. In a very short time they
find that they have a child who "makes a fuss" every night before going
to bed in order to see if his parents will let him stay up a half hour
longer. This all results from the fact that the parents have been inconsistent in their pay-offs. They've put the child on a partial pay-off
schedule. He's learned that if he "makes a fuss" before going to bed,
there's a chance he may get to stay up for a half hour longer. It doesn't
pay-off all the time, but frequently enough to make him want to try
for the extra half hour every night by "making a fuss." Besides, it's fun
to play such tug-of-war games with parents.

30. Another way of saying that parents have the

child on a partial pay-off schedule is to say they

are _____ in their payoffs.

---

29. partial

30. inconsistent

31. What his parents in essence are doing is

_____ his whining and pestering

behavior on a _____

schedule.

32. This actually makes it stronger and more likely

to _____.

Shaping

The last principle that we want to discuss is called Shaping. This principle states that complex behavior can be learned most easily by breaking it into small steps or single responses.

Instead of expecting a child to perform a complex behavioral response on his first few attempts a *shaping* approach should be used. The task should be analyzed and an attempt made to determine the various steps or parts of which it consists. We then arrange these parts of the response in a series. We place them in a natural order from the most basic or elementary part of the behavior proceeding through in step-wise fashion to the complete response. Each part requires a little more of the child than the one preceding. The child performs the first part of the response. After he is performing this part easily, we require the next step. Again, he is given time to learn this part of it well. Additional steps are required until he has been gradually shaped into performing the complex behavior or task. Of course, it is understood that each step or unit is followed by a *reward*.

33. An organism can best learn a complex response

if it is presented to him in easy _____,

each one building on the previous response.

34. In _____ a response, liberal use

should be made of _____ at each step

along the way.

---

31. rewarding   32. continue (persist)   34. shaping
    partial   33. steps (units)   rewards

This approach is used in animal training. The complex behaviors that the trained dogs, elephants, horses, etc., perform are shaped in just this manner.

An Animal Study Illustrating the Principle of "Shaping"

Pigeons have been taught to go through very unusual and amusing routines by this method of shaping. In one case a pigeon was trained to peck at a light and turn a complete circle before receiving a grain of corn. This was simply done by breaking this task down into many simple steps. In the first step the pigeon received a grain of corn if he turned his head slightly to the side and back before pecking at the light. After the pigeon was performing this task very well, the trainer merely required him to turn his head a little more to the side. Slowly the pigeon learned to turn a half circle and then turn back before pecking at the light and receiving a grain of corn. After this response was well trained the pigeon was then expected to make the circle complete rather than turn back at the half way point. Soon the pigeon was making circles constantly before pecking at the light and eating the corn. Two pigeons have even been shaped into playing ping pong in order to obtain food.

35. In this example, the pigeon learned to turn a circle by means of a _____ approach.

36. This was done by breaking this difficult task (for a pigeon at least) into many _____.

An Example of How Inappropriate Behaviors May Be "Shaped"

The way in which this principle operates to increase the intensity of inappropriate responses in children can be illustrated by the previous example we presented of a child pestering and whining to stay up and watch TV past the regular hour. We've already seen how inconsistently rewarding the child by letting him stay up past the bed time can cause this behavior to become a nightly occurrence. (Principle of partial scheduling.) The principle of shaping can also explain how these "fusses" the child makes can become more intense or severe with each passing night. Initially the child may only make a fuss for a short while and we give in. The next evening he may try again but we don't give in and he goes to bed. The next evening he persists for just a little longer and gets a little more upset. We eventually give in just to have peace and quiet so

---

35. shaping   36. simple steps

we can watch our program. The next night we insist he go to bed, but he really puts up a fuss. Before we know it a half hour has passed. We've been distracted from our program and the child has managed to stay up. And so it continues; the child being shaped into increasing the severity of his "fussing behavior" each night because we eventually give in. The whining and pestering eventually are *shaped* into real tantrums that take place every night at bed time. At this point, father throws up his arms and says, "What did I do to deserve this?"

37. If a small fuss does not earn the _____
a larger fuss is gradually _____.

38. The four principles which influence our ability
to learn are:

1) _____
2) _____
3) _____
4) _____

39. The reason for interspersing questions throughout these chapters is consistent with the principle of: _____.

These four principles, along with the "law of reinforcement," are very powerful tools for understanding and explaining how behavior is learned. Failure to recognize these principles operating in our lives and to apply them correctly is responsible for many of the behavioral problems encountered in the mental health field. When these principles are understood and used correctly by parents, teachers, mental health care-givers, etc. many so-called "personality problems" disappear.

---

37. reward
    shaped
38. timing
    pairing
    scheduling
    shaping

39. timing—the immediacy of feedback for
    improved learning. (The questions are
    presented with the answers given so you
    can get immediate knowledge of results.
    This is similar to the way teaching
    material is presented in the teaching
    machines discussed on page 25.)

4 Observing and Recording Behavior

We studied in the previous chapters the basic principles of behavior and how an understanding and correct use of these principles can bring about changes in behavior.

In this chapter we want to help you get started in actually learning the skills and techniques of making behavioral changes. There are very definite steps one should follow in planning for effective and meaningful behavioral changes.

1. In planning for behavioral change there are

_____ one should follow.

Achieving a change in behavior can mean a number of things. In the approach being presented here, change will mean a change in the *frequency* of a behavior. The number of times the individual performs the behavior may increase or decrease. Or to say it another way: The individual can be trained to repeat the behavior more often or to repeat it less often.

2. In this chapter we are going to be concerned

with attempts to bring about a _____

in the _____ of a behavior.

_____

1. definite steps   2. change
                               frequency

The very first step in starting a program to change behavior is careful and controlled observation of the behavior as it is presently occurring. We must observe what is going on now before we can set behavior goals or make plans for achieving them.

3. The first step in changing any behavior is careful and controlled _____ of the behavior.

To get changes in the frequency of a behavior we must first make a study of the present problem situation. This means we must record the exact frequency with which the behavior is occurring under present conditions. This helps us decide (1) just how much of a problem the behavior really is, and (2) how effective our procedures are once we start our program for change.

4. In order to know how to change behavior we need to know its _____ under _____ conditions.

There is also another reason why we should make a careful record of how frequently a behavior occurs. Our mind has a tendency to see things to fit our personal desires. Many times we over- or under-estimate the frequency of behavior. We may find it unpleasant or disturbing (over-estimate) or we don't want to admit a problem really exists (under-estimate).

5. We make careful _____ of behavior in order to be sure things are the way we say they are.

A group of school aged children were being observed and one of the research assistants noted that one child had what appeared to him to be a great amount of "oral" behavior. He was always putting things into his mouth, touching his lips, etc. The assistant expressed concern that the child was emotionally disturbed and needed psychological help. Before acting upon this concern the senior researcher asked that data be gathered on the number of times such "oral" responses occurred, not

---

3. observation   present
4. frequency (occurrence)   5. records (observations)

only in this one child, but on all the other children in the room as well. Using a special procedure, the frequency of oral behaviors for all the children in the class were observed and recorded. An oral behavior was defined as "placing objects or fingers against the lips or touching any part of the inside of the mouth with any object or finger."

The observations were made and the frequency of these behaviors totaled. It was discovered that the child which the research assistant thought had a very high (and hence abnormal) frequency of oral behavior was actually no different from other children. Through *careful observation* it was noted that all children engage in "oral" behaviors to some extent. The frequency of this one child's "oral" behavior was not any greater than that of the other children.

6. Careful observation of "oral" responses in a group of children showed the research assistant to be _____ in believing that one child had a very high frequency of such behaviors.

Parents, who find their child's behavior intolerable, tend to over-estimate the actual frequency of its occurrence. There are, on the other hand, parents who do not want to admit that their child has problems. They deny the frequency with which a behavior is occurring. Thus, it is very important to make careful observations of the behaviors that are of concern to us by attempting to count how frequently they occur.

7. We make careful _____ of _____ in order to be sure the behavior occurs as frequently as we say or believe it does.

In the previous chapters, we presented scientific principles of behavior. Now we want to train you in following a scientific approach to using these scientific principles. The first step in any scientific investigation is careful observation and recording.

8. The _____ step in any scientific investigation is careful _____.

---

6. incorrect (wrong)
7. observations
   behavior

8. first
   observation and recording

Defining a Particular Behavior You Want To Study

In order to make these observations as accurate, objective, and useful as possible, we need to specify exactly what the behavior is we are going to record or count. We need to determine the parts that make up the behavior. We did this in the preceding example where we define "oral" behavior as "placing objects or fingers against the lips or touching any part of the inside of the mouth with any object or finger."

9. We _____ oral behavior as "placing objects or fingers against the lips or touching any part of the inside of the mouth with any object or finger."

In most cases you won't need such a fancy name for the behavior. You may just want to count how many times a temper tantrum occurs, how many times Timmy hits his sister, or the frequency of curse words Billy is using (and most certainly picked up from the neighbor's kids!). But even here, it helps to get a clear understanding of just what goes to make up the behavior you feel needs correcting. Before we can count the behavior we must know what it is.

10. Before we count a behavior we must _____ what it is we are counting.

Having decided that some behavior needs changing, but before we set up a program to make the change, we first (1) clearly indicate what the present behavior is we want to change, and (2) count the frequency with which it is presently occurring.

"Before" and "After" Observations

In order to understand all the conditions effecting the behavior, there are two additional things we should do. While observing the behavior we should also determine (1) what happens just before the

9. defined
10. know (define) (understand)

behavior occurs, and (2) what happens immediately following the
behavior. To put it another way: (1) what is it that sets the behavior off, and (2) what happens as a result of the behavior?

11. While observing behavior, we also note what

happens ———————— and ————————

it occurs.

We said in Chapter 3 that the law of reinforcement tells us that any behavior that occurs repeatedly must be receiving a reward. We, therefore, want to carefully observe what events follow the behavior so we can make a guess at what is rewarding the behavior and keeping it going.

12. Observing what happens after a response occurs

may help us determine what the ————————

for it is.

HELPFUL INFORMATION	SCIENTIFIC APPROACH	HELPFUL INFORMATION
What happens before the behavior occurs? What set it off?	Careful observation & recording of the frequency of the behavior.	What happens after the behavior? What could be the reward?

13. The scientific approach to understanding be-

havior requires ————————————

————————————————————

————————————————————.

Recording Behavior

The charts at the end of this chapter can be used to help you in following a scientific approach to behavior change. To show how it is done, we have chosen to record the frequency of temper tantrums in a child called Ronnie (see Figure 1, pp. 51–52).

---

11. before
    after
12. reward

13. careful observation and
    recording of the frequency
    of a behavior

At the bottom of Figure 1 (left side) we have clearly defined the behavior we are going to observe and record. On the right hand side of this chart we have listed the days of the week. Each day is broken down into two-hour periods to cover 24 hours. We can then place a mark (1) in the appropriate space whenever the behavior is observed to occur.

14. According to our chart, a temper tantrum from

Ronnie is defined as: ———————————

———————————————————

———————————————————.

In our example, during the first week of observation and recording, Ronnie had one temper tantrum between 7-9 p.m. on Sunday, one between 9-11 a.m. on Wednesday and one between 9-11 a.m. on Saturday.

15. During the second week Ronnie had two temper

tantrums; one between 7-9 on Sunday, one be-

tween ——————— a.m. on ———————————.

Obtaining Baseline Data

We then add up these occurrences and get a count of how much this behavior occurs under regular conditions on a weekly basis. In this instance, since the frequencies are so low, we will just take the weekly average which comes to 2.5. This count of how much a behavior occurs under present conditions is called a *baseline*. The baseline frequency of a behavior tells us where we are beginning with the behavior and how serious it really is.

16. A record of the frequency of a behavior before

anything is done to change it is called a

———————————————————.

14. screams repeatedly, throws things or falls on floor, continuous screaming and thrashing about.

15. 9:00 - 11:00
Wednesday

16. baseline

On the left hand side of the chart you will observe two columns, one labeled "Before" and the other "After." The first column reminds us to observe what happened before the behavior occurred. What may have set it off? The second column reminds us to observe what events followed the behavior. What may have rewarded it? Concerning Ronnie's temper tantrums we note:

BEFORE	BEHAVIOR	AFTER
Asks for something and is refused. Mother and other people present.	Tantrum behavior is occurring 2.5 times per week.	Usually gets all or part of what he asks for.

17. According to the preceding information Ronnie's _____ for temper tantrums was 2.5 per week.

18. They appear to occur when Ronnie _____
    _____
    _____.

Thus our chart tells us that Ronnie has 2 or 3 temper tantrums per week. They appear to be set off by a situation where Ronnie, in the presence of others, asks for something from his mother and is refused. The result is that he generally ends up getting all or part of what he wanted. This is probably the reward.

19. Ronnie's reward for temper tantrums is probably _____
    _____.

We have zeroed in on the behavior by obtaining a *baseline* of its present frequency. We have also obtained some knowledge into what situations set off the behavior and what results follow (and probably reward) the behavior. We can now consider a program for changing it.

---

17. baseline

18. asks for something and is refused.

19. getting all or part of what he wants

20. Having obtained a ———————— on a behavior

and determined what happens ———————— and

———————— it occurs, we can now consider

changing it.

Changing Behavior

Do we desire to increase the frequency or decrease the frequency of this behavior? How much? In our present example, it is certain that we want to decrease its frequency. We would like to be able to eliminate it completely by bringing the frequency down to zero.

21. We will most certainly want to bring the fre-

quency of inappropriate or undesirable behavior

down to ————————————————.

There are two ways to make a behavior change. Looking at our chart we see that two things can be changed. We can change the "Before" side or the "After" side. We can change the physical or social situation that sets off the behavior or we can change what happens after the behavior. We can withdraw the reward supporting the behavior.

22. Behavior can be changed by changing what

happens ———————— or what happens————————

the behavior.

A Case of Temper Tantrums

Ronnie's temper tantrums occur at the grocery store in the presence of strangers, or at bedtime when father is there, after he has asked mother for something and she refuses. We could probably get rid of some of the

---

20. baseline   21. zero
     before   22. before
     after   after (following)

temper tantrums by (1) granting Ronnie his request as soon as he asks, (2) not taking Ronnie to the grocery store, (3) letting him stay up until he is ready to go to bed himself. What would happen if we followed any of these three approaches? We must decide if it is reasonable to let Ronnie have whatever he asks for in the grocery store and stay up later than regular bedtime if he so desires. Obviously, this does not sound like a good way to raise Ronnie, so we can reject these two alternatives. The second approach was for mother to leave Ronnie at home when she goes to the store. This may be hard to do as mother would have to get a sitter to watch Ronnie while she is at the store. It looks like changing these conditions in order to change the behavior is not a very practical approach.

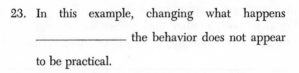

23. In this example, changing what happens _____ the behavior does not appear to be practical.

Let us now look at what follows the behavior. Since the behavior is occurring with some frequency there must be a reward supporting it. It seems that in this situation the reward for Ronnie's temper tantrums is getting all or part of his request. Another reward may be the control he has over his parents by upsetting them. One way to handle the problem might be to stop giving in to Ronnie when he has a temper tantrum and not to get upset. One could ignore the temper tantrum itself. In this way we attempt to end the behavior by withholding the rewards that support it.

24. One way to eliminate Ronnie's temper tantrums is to withhold _____ from them.

One way to prevent Ronnie's bedtime temper tantrums might be to increase his desire to go to bed by making it a very pleasant event. Father could carry him to bed and give him special attention. He might even read a story to him until he falls asleep. Attention would be put on "having a story read" and not "going to bed." In other words, father could tell Ronnie that it's time to have a story read to him but first he must be in bed. Of course, parents have to have enough interest in the child's wel-being to be willing to give up waching TV to read to him. Whenever we separate ourselves physically from the rewarding situation we lose

---

23. before

24. rewards

46 the opportunity of increasing our value or importance to our children through the principle of pairing.

> 25. One way to eliminate temper tantrums at bed
>
> time might be to make going to bed ——————
>
> by reading a story to Ronnie.

Mother might end temper tantrums in the grocery store by letting Ronnie help her plan desserts for meals. She could then give him his own shopping list with all the desserts listed on it and permit him to pick them off the shelf and place them in the cart at the store. In this way she can make him feel like he is buying some of the things he wants. He is also getting the attention of mother as he becomes a helper on the shopping trip. Both mother and father would also want to make it a point to compliment Ron on his excellent choice of dessert at each meal.

> 26. In this example mother is substituting ————
>
> ——————————————for Ronnie's asking for some
>
> item for himself.

A Case of Brother Hitting Sister

Teddy is a rather difficult child these days. He has a problem that is also annoying his parents. It seems to occur all the time.

Teddy has taken to hitting his little sister and pushing her. She has fallen down and occasionally been bruised or scratched. Mother is at her wit's end about what to do. It seems to continue in spite of her efforts to scold or punish him.

This behavior occurs several times each day. For such high frequency behavior we use Figure 2 (see page 53). On this chart the frequency of the behavior can be recorded for up to 50 times a day. It is divided into two sections. The first 10 spaces starting at the left are for 10 days of *baseline data*. The rest of the spaces are for recording the changes in the frequency of the behavior *after* we have started our program for change. Every time the behavior occurs a space in the column for that day can be X'd in.

---

25. rewarding (pleasant) (desirable)

26. planning and picking out desserts

27. According to our chart, on day 5 of the base-line period, Teddy hit his sister ——————— times.

28. The behavior we are observing is defined as:

———————————————————————————

———————————————————————————.

Because of the frequency with which this behavior is occurring, it would be difficult to make a report of each situation that came before and followed the response. So we don't do it every time, but perhaps two or three times a day. These can be reported on the back side of the chart.

29. Although it is difficult to record every instance, due to the frequency of this behavior, one should pay attention to what happens ———————

———————————————————————————.

After 10 days of careful observing and recording, a baseline of Teddy's hitting his little sister should be obtained. We add up the total number of times Teddy hit his sister during the 10-day period and divide by ten. This gives us the average number of times Teddy hit his sister each day. We then write up our findings.

BEFORE	HITTING SISTER	AFTER
Teddy and his sister are in their home. Mother and/or father present.	Average of 4 times per day.	Mother generally scolds Teddy, sometimes a quiet lecture. On 2 occasions, sent to room; 2 other occasions, was spanked.

30. The ——————— for Teddy's behavior averages 4 times per day.

31. This represents the average frequency of this behavior per day over a ————— day period.

---

27. four

28. hits or pushes his little sister so that she falls

29. before and after the behavior

30. baseline   31. ten

It is clear that this behavior needs to be reduced to zero occurrences. What can be done to control this behavior? The conditions under which the behavior occurs suggests that one approach might be to keep Teddy and his sister separated. This however, seems a little ridiculous.

The other approach would be to withhold the reward. On the face of it, it would seem that there is no reward (unless it is sister's cries for help) because Teddy frequently gets punished whenever he is confronted with his willful act of aggression toward his sister. However, it is evident that while Teddy is being punished for this behavior he is also receiving a lot of attention and this may be the reward supporting the behavior. Mother stops whatever she is doing and comes to Teddy to scold or correct him. Poor sister usually goes unnoticed except for a comforting pat or word. Teddy might even be dragged off to his room and told to remain there until he can be good. He is really controlling mother by stopping her activities and upsetting her.

> 32. The most likely reward supporting Teddy's hitting and pushing his sister is ——————————— from mother.

Completely ignoring the behavior would not be wise as sister might get seriously hurt if mother continues to ignore Teddy's hitting her. He just might start hitting sister harder and harder in order to get her attention.

> 33. In this situation, if mother paid attention to Teddy after he has started hitting his sister harder she would be ——————————— a more intense hitting response. (Recall the appropriate principle at work here.)

One approach might be to give the same amount of attention to reward the response of "playing cooperatively and helpfully with his sister." This suggests that the situation might be handled by rewarding

---

32. attention
33. shaping

Teddy with praise, attention, plus a special treat (cookies, juice, toy)
for helping or playing cooperatively with sister. Mother might begin
with a situation where she is present in the room. She could control the
play between the two children and praise Teddy every time he does
something nice for his sister. She might sit them down together for
cookies and juice at the end of the play session. She might let Teddy buy
a small toy on a day when he's played especially well with his sister.
Gradually mother can withdraw more and more from the situation as
Teddy's aggressive behavior toward sister ceases.

34. In this example, a special treat was ――――――
with praise and attention in order to reward
the response of ――――――――――――――
――――――――――――――――――――――――.

35. Mother's withdrawing gradually from the situation as Teddy's aggression ceases illustrates the
principle of ――――――――――――――.

A *combination* of both approaches (1) ignoring the hitting
behavior when it occurs and (2) building up cooperative and helpful
responses by setting up situations where it can be rewarded with
attention and praise seems like the best way to handle such a
situation. (For another way to handle this situation, refer to the
discussion on pages 70–71.)

36. A double-barreled approach to changing some
behavior is to ―――――――― the undesirable
behavior while, at the same time, rewarding a
―――――――― behavior.

Let's assume it was decided to do just that. We can see what progress
was made by looking at the chart. The frequency of Teddy's "hitting
sister" begins to drop quickly. On the eleventh day it did not occur even
once. After that there were a few occurrences but nothing to be very
concerned about. In fact, from our chart we see that the increase in this
behavior on days 12 and 13 happened as a result of a cold that made him
irritable and upset. Unusual events in the child's life sometimes cause
inappropriate behavior to return.

---

34. paired   36. ignore
    playing cooperatively with sister   desired (appropriate)

35. scheduling

37. According to our chart, another slight increase

occurred in Teddy's pushing behavior as a result

of a ———————————————.

Perhaps he was jealous of the attention his mother gave to all the other children.

We have recorded our results and brought an end to a most unpleasant behavior. Mother should feel much satisfaction over the success of this project. She might even put the chart in the family album!

At this point, if you have done your reading seriously and answered the question frames conscientiously, you should have a good basic understanding of behavioral science. You have been introduced to the basic laws or principles which effect behavior and given practical examples of how they work in our everyday lives. You have been given a short introduction to how to go about making behavioral changes based on the scientific approach of observing and recording data. You have been informed of the potency of giving and withholding rewards (especially attention) in effecting behavioral changes. It is now up to you to get to work planning programs whereby you can change the behavior of those around you, hopefully for the better. If you continue reading in this manual you will see how these principles have actually been used in clinical settings to treat behavioral problems and deficits.

---

37. birthday party

CHILD'S NAME   Ronnie B. (age 4)   WEEK I   DATE   Jan. 5-12

BEFORE (Where? Who was present? What were they doing?)	AFTER (How did situation change as a result?)		SUN.	MON.	TUES.	WED.	THURS.	FRI.	SAT.	TOTAL
						(Days of the Week)				
(2) Wednesday — In the grocery store Mother had refused to let him ride in cart full of groceries. Others present.	Mother rearranged packages so that seat could be utilized and put him in the cart. Others smiled.	7-9								
		9-11				(2) 1			(3) 1	
(3) Saturday — In grocery store Mother refused to buy candy bar Ronnie had picked up. Check out clerk & others in line.	Mother quickly includes candy in pile of groceries being checked out. Others & clerk watch with interest.	11-1								
		1-3								
		3-5								
		5-7								
(1) Sunday — In living room. Mr. & Mrs. B. present. Mr. & Mrs. B. watching TV — Mrs. B. attempting to take Ronnie to bed.	Bedtime is 7 p.m., Ronnie was carried to bed at 7:30 by his father and told to stay there. Father angry, mother complaining.	7-9	(1) 1							
		9-11								
		11-1								
		1-3								
		3-5								
		5-7								

DEFINE THE BEHAVIOR HERE: (be precise)

Tantrum behavior. Ronnie screams repeatedly, throwing things or falling to the floor to continue screaming and thrashing about.

FIGURE 1. CONT.

CHILD'S NAME Ronnie B. (age 4)   WEEK II   DATE   Jan. 13-19

BEFORE (Where? Who was present? What were they doing?)	AFTER (How did situation change as a result?)		(Days of the Week)							
			SUN.	MON.	TUES.	WED.	THURS.	FRI.	SAT.	TOTAL
(2) Wednesday — In grocery store. Refused to buy him box of animal crackers.	Mother shows large box of cookies she intends to buy and lets him carry them about the store.	7-9								
		9-11				(2) 1				
		11-1								
		1-3								
		3-5								
		5-7								
(1) Sunday — Mrs. B. watching TV in living room. Ronnie given a bath and Mother attempted to put directly to bed.	Mother lets Ronnie come to living room to say good night to Father and sit up for a half-hour longer.	7-9 (1) 1								
		9-11								
		11-1								
		1-3								
		3-5								
		5-7								

CHILD'S NAME: TEDDY R. (age 5)

DATES: January 5 to March 6

INSTANCES OF THE BEHAVIOR

DAYS

{BASELINE}

INTRODUCE PROGRAM AT THIS POINT

(PROGRAM FOR CHANGE)

Teddy has a cold, not feeling very well, irritable and upset.

Birthday Party

Program begun on January 5.

Program to be followed

Ignore Teddy's hitting behavior.

Set up situations where Teddy can be rewarded for playing appropriately with his sister.

Behavior Defined: Hits or pushes his little sister so that she falls.

Part II

Clinical Applications of Behavioral Laws

A case history taken from: Thorne, Gaylord L., Tharp, Roland G., Wetzel, Ralph J.; "Behavior Modification Techniques: New Tools for Probation Officers"; *Federal Probation;* Vol. 31; No. 2, June, 1967; pp. 21—27. (Slight changes or modifications have been made in the text of this case history so that it would be easily understandable to the audience to whom this manual is directed, persons with no previous background in scientific behavior theory.)

Mark is a 7th grade boy referred by the local juvenile court for (1) refusing to do chores, disobedience and defiance, (2) impulsively destroying toys and family property, (3) stealing both at home and at school, and (4) poor relations with friends and school mates and frequent fighting with his two younger sisters.

Mark's father handles all discipline problems with a combination of extended lectures and punishment. His whippings are often followed by another destructive act by Mark, but he still continues to rely upon physical punishment to keep Mark in line. Mark's mother tends to lecture him after his misbehaviors and is uncertain and inconsistent in her expectations of him. Mark's destructive acts around the home had gotten to the point where they needed immediate attention.

Mark's allowance was completely dependent upon above average report card grades. This meant long periods of no reward for Mark as his report card was very poor indeed.

The parents were counseled into making his allowance dependent upon nondestructive behavior at home rather than on his report card. If he did destroy or damage something, he would lose money for that day, plus having to pay for the repairs. In addition, Mark could earn points each day for the successful completion of chores at home, points that would accumulate toward the purchase of a bicycle in about six months. Regular assignments were encouraged from school so that Mark could be rewarded for studying at least 30 minutes after school. When father would arrive home from work he praised Mark for studying. If Mark studied each day of the week father would give him a bonus of either an increase in his allowance or a special weekend outing with him. Father was to ignore Mark on any day that he did not study. Both parents kept daily records on these behaviors.

At the end of seven weeks Mark had not committed a single destructive act, there had been no reports of stealing, he rarely missed completing a day of chores, and he was studying at least one-half hour six nights a week.

His parents were most pleased but surprised the therapist by stating that they did not feel that Mark should be praised and rewarded for appropriate acts. This just amounted to "bribery!" It was unacceptable to Mark's parents to use rewards to shape behavior. This point was, in fact, so distressing to them that they were seriously considering dropping the program despite its considerable success. Fortunately, report cards came out at this time and Mark showed improvement in both study and behavior grades. This made it possible to persuade them to continue.

A disaster occurred several weeks later which almost ended the program once and for all! Mark broke his eyeglasses. This prevented any studying for a week, but worse still it upset Mark's father because of the expense. Mark was verbally reprimanded and his bicycle point chart was done away with.

Six weeks passed before any consistent plan of action was reinstated. School work, occasionally rewarded with father's praise, was maintained at its high level. Two minor acts of destructiveness occurred at home (breaking a bath room tile and a toy) and he exhibited some defiant behaviors toward his mother. Mark's completion of chores began to drop. This, more than anything else, brought the parents back for advice. They accepted the suggestion to again make a chart for the chores and reward completion of them. The only reward the parents would accept, however, was interaction with the father and his praise. Earning money and the bicycle were still not allowed by the parents.

About five weeks were spent in keeping a daily chart on Mark's completion of chores. He would place a star on the chart and then the parents would praise him. The frequency of chore completion soon rose to 100 percent and this so pleased the father he decided to reinstate the bicycle point-chart. Completion of chores and obedient behaviors would then earn points and when a set number was accumulated he would get a new bicycle. Mark earned his new bicycle in thirty-four days!

Mark's parents are now fully convinced of the importance of making rewards dependent upon behavior and the effectiveness of shaping behavior with rewards. A six week follow-up shows no return to previous misbehaviors. In the beginning Mark had made two D's and an F on his midterm report card. His final report card had no mark below a C.

such behaviors by responding with a well-placed swat or a verbal
complaint ("Don't do that," "Can't you behave," "I'm going to swat your
little behind if you don't calm down," etc.)

4. Behavior problems often develop in children

where the parents take _____

behavior for granted and punish or attend to

_____ behavior.

Consider for a minute your own behavior toward your young child
while talking on the telephone. Have you ever at the end of your phone
call complimented your child for his/her quiet, non-disrupting behavior
which permitted you to talk without any distractions or interference?
Chances are that when you are occupied on the phone such behaviors
go ignored. On the other hand, if the child is making noises or doing
other things that you don't like you interrupt your conversation to ask
him to be quiet, threaten to punish him or actually leave the phone
to deliver the corrective blow. This example shows just one of the many
everyday situations that indicate our tendency to take for granted and
ignore appropriate behavioral responses and call attention to and punish
inappropriate responses.

5. Parents are generally quick to _____

children whose behavior does not fulfill their

expectations.

6. The well-behaved child generally goes _____.

Reversing the "Pay-offs"

The emphasis in this manual so far has been that two of the most
powerful tools for shaping children's behavior are *attention,* on the one
hand, and *ignoring* on the other. Generally speaking, attention is rewarding and leads to a repetition or an increase in the frequency of responses
which bring it about and inattention or being ignored is a punishment
which leads to a decrease in the frequency of those responses, which it
follows.

Extinction

---

4. appropriate (desirable)   5. punish
   inappropriate (undesirable)   6. ignored

7. If a parent desires a behavior to occur more often, he should _____ to it.

8. Behavior a parent wishes not to occur should be _____.

This being the case then two very strong influences are at work in the life of a child growing up in such homes. Behaviors which are desirable or appropriate are ignored and hence, not rewarded, while inappropriate or undesirable behaviors are attended to and hence *rewarded*. This attention may be associated with physical punishment such as spanking the child, but we are still, at the same time, *rewarding* the child with attention. The child is also learning that he can control the parent's behavior by misbehaving. So although we believe we are punishing the child, we may actually be rewarding him. This *reward of attention* and control over the parent may have greater effect on the behavior than the expected punishment.

9. Punishment is often not very effective because the _____ connected with it is very rewarding.

As a result of the "pay-off" schedule outlined above, the child acquires the idea that certain behaviors don't pay-off because parents just go about their own business and overlook them. But other behaviors get parents upset, disrupt their routines, throw them into a turmoil and make them do all kinds of irrational things, including spanking children.

10. Exerting _____ over the behavior of one's parents may be rewarding to a small child.

The child thus discovers that he has a great deal of control over his parents' actions by doing certain things. For the young child who is testing his environment and investigating ways to change it, the experience of parents getting upset over something he does may lead him to repeat it just to find out if it has the same effect again and again and again. Before one knows it, the parents and the child may find themselves caught in a struggle to see who will give in first.

11. Getting parents _____ may be rewarding to the child who is testing his environment.

---

7. attend   9. attention   11. upset

8. ignored   10. control

It may be because of this that we get some of the unexpected results in the disciplining of our children. Those parents who spend most of the time ignoring their children unless they are doing things they cannot tolerate may find such behaviors persisting or increasing rather than decreasing in frequency. More than one parent has been heard to say, "I've disciplined the child severely and he still refuses to mind, in fact, he appears to get worse." In such a situation, it may be that the reward of attention and control over the parents that the child receives from such behaviors far exceeds the influence of any repressive steps the parents may be using to stop the behavior. For the child who craves attention and recognition, unpleasant attention and recognition may be more desirable than no attention or recognition at all.

> 12. Discipline may fail to eliminate a behavior because the child craves the _____ more than he fears the punishment.

Treating the Child With Behavioral Problems

Many behaviorally disordered children end up being referred for treatment because their parents can no longer tolerate them. The parents are at a loss as to how such behaviors developed and even more at a loss as to how to correct the situation. Everything they do seems to make it worse. So they turn for help to professionals. This may result in the child being placed in an institution, separating him from his family.

In order to correct the behavior of such children by the proper use of behavioral laws, many facilities dealing with behaviorally disordered children have established a total environmental approach to the problem. In such facilities a procedure is set up whereby the laws of behavior can be correctly applied; in fact, applied so effectively that one can overcome in a few months behavior problems that may have been supported by six, eight, or ten years of inappropriate reward schedules. It is a system whereby the treatment staff in such a setting can use a combination of praise and "tokens" to reward children for appropriate behavior patterns and withhold attention and "tokens" for the inappropriate behaviors which require their being placed there.

12. attention

13. Some treatment facilities are now attempting to correct problem behaviors in children through correct use of _____.

14. In such treatment centers they teach behaviorally disordered children appropriate behavior patterns by means of _____ paired with "tokens."

Tokens

The "tokens" children are given in such a setting may consist of colored chips, plastic strips, metal discs, etc., anything that can be easily given to the child at the time he is engaged in appropriate behavior. These tokens can be used by the children to buy many basic necessities and all of the luxuries that are available to them at the treatment center. For example, tokens may be used to buy seconds on meals and desserts. A toy library may be set up where the children can pay tokens to rent a toy to play with for an hour. Usually a canteen is available where the children can buy between-meal snacks, small toys, books and other such desirable items. Special activities or events such as movies, swimming, horseback riding, etc. can be obtained with a certain number of tokens. In general, such settings provide the child with the basic necessities for living free. Additional pleasures can be obtained with the "tokens" the child has earned.

Tokens are earned by the child simply by engaging in appropriate or desirable behaviors—those behaviors which the treatment staff (after discussing the child's problems) feel are necessary to make this child well-adjusted in his home and school. In addition, every time the token is given, the child is told why he is receiving the token. In this way, a physical reward is paired with a social reward. On the other hand, if the child has used inappropriate behavior he is ignored and given no tokens. Hence, when it comes time to go to the canteen or participate in special activities, he won't have enough tokens and will thus be unable to participate in the activity or buy anything at the canteen. This illustrates to him the value of constructive behavior.

15. Tokens are earned simply by engaging in _____ behaviors.

---

13. behavioral laws (behavioral principles)   15. appropriate

14. praise

16. If the child behaves inappropriately, he is ——————, hence he earns no ——————.

17. Whenever a token is given, the child is also told why he is getting the token. This represents the principle of ——————————.

Reasons Why Tokens Are Used

The use of tokens, in addition to the verbal praise and attention, is made necessary for two reasons. In the first place, many of the children who come to mental health facilities for treatment are so accustomed to getting "paid off" for inappropriate or unacceptable behavior that they may not respond quickly to simple attention and praise for appropriate behavior. A token, however, soon comes to be desired by the child because it can be used to buy food, toys, special activities, etc. Thus, in order to make speedy changes in the behavior of these children and increase the value of social rewards, it is often necessary to pair (following sound behavioral principles) the social reward (verbal praise and attention) with a physical reward (indicated by the token).

18. One reason tokens are used in retraining children is to bring about a change more

——————————————————.

Secondly, requiring a staff member to give a child a token for appropriate behaviors, assists the staff member in making a definite response to the child and focusing attention on him and the appropriate behavior. If a staff member were merely required to say something to the child, the staff member may forget or he might feel too tired to make the effort. But since the child needs tokens to get things the staff member must be ready to respond to those behaviors of the child which deserve rewards. Otherwise, the child could not function very well in the program.

---

16. ignored tokens   17. pairing   18. quickly

19. Tokens are also used to be sure that the staff

member _____ to the child.

Thus, tokens are used not only because they are powerful rewards to the child, but they are a reminder to the staff to "be alert" to situations where tokens can be given.

Examples Illustrating the Inappropriate Approach to Inappropriate Behaviors

Before these programs were developed the approach to behavior in many such facilities was much the same as in the home itself. Inappropriate or deviant behavior was attended to and acceptable or appropriate behavior was overlooked. Following are some typical examples to illustrate this point.

Disrupting Behavior

A group of children are clustered around an aide absorbed in a story she is reading them. They are well-behaved, quiet, attentive, etc. After several minutes one child engages in behavior that disrupts the other children and interferes with the listening situation. Another child leaves the group and looks for mischief elsewhere. The normal response is for one or more staff members to respond to this situation by directing their attention to the two problem children. Scolds, reprimands, lectures, physical restraints are only a few of the controlling responses that might be used to bring these two "deviants" back into line. The child preventing the other children from enjoying story-time might be held immobile on a staff member's lap (arms clutched tightly around him!) to prevent him from disrupting the other children or he may be carried off to his room. The child who has wandered off to another part of the building may be threatened with unpleasant consequences if he does not return or forcibly returned to the group if he persists in ignoring the staff member's warning.

19. responds (attends)

From our previous discussion you can see all too clearly what is happening. The children quietly and attentively listening to the story read are ignored. The misbehaving children, on the other hand, are getting attention and exercising control over the staff as well as over the other children. The staff interrupts whatever they are doing to "control" them. They invest time and effort in restraining them in their lap, removing them to their room, talking to them, etc. In essence, the staff's behavior is being controlled by these children rather than the other way around. These children have learned that "acting out" behavior is a way to force a staff member and the other children to stop what they are doing and pay *attention* to them. Soon all the children begin to see that the only way to get status in the group and attention from staff (the only way to be an important person) is to misbehave from expected norms. They see the disrupting child successfully get the staff members' attention. They, in turn, may model their own behavior after this child to get attention also. So we see that the impulsive manner in which we attempt to control disturbing children may actually serve to increase the very behaviors we wish to eliminate.

> 20. The way most treatment approaches are carried
>
>   out, disrupting children receive more—————
>
>   from staff members than well-behaved children.

Aggressing Behavior

A second illustration of how pay-offs can be misapplied is the situation where one child is physically aggressive toward another child. Typically the adult responds by verbally reprimanding and/or physically restraining the aggressing child. He may even be dragged off to his room and given a thorough lecture. The unfortunate child who has been attacked goes unattended, or at most, receives only a passing word of sympathy. Here again, it is the misbehaving child that receives the major portion of the attention and exercises control over the situation.

> 21. When one child attacks another child, it is usu-
>
>   ally the ——————————— child that gets
>
>   most of the attention.

---

20. attention

21. attacking

Another misapplication of the laws of behavior is sometimes seen in the behavior of the staff toward those children who refuse to participate in activities with other children. Working with disordered children, it is a common experience to have one or two that do not want to participate in group activities with the rest of the children. For example, if a group of children go to the gym to play badminton there may be one or two children who refuse to participate. They linger on the outskirts of the game, sit along the side of the gym, or find something else to occupy their time. The staff attempts to encourage their interest in the game, but they refuse so the game proceeds without them. The staff members, however, feel it is untherapeutic for a child to exclude himself from such interactions. They may leave the game to reassure the child his participation in the game is desired and attempt to encourage him to participate. The typical approach is to tell him how much fun the other children are having or how happy they would be if he participated, etc. Generally, such appeals to reason or emotion fail and the staff member reluctantly returns to the game only to try again later. Before the activity ends such children may be approached several times in attempts to get them to participate.

22.   Children who refuse to participate in group ac-

tivities often are the center of _____.

The other children who are participating in the activity are, of course, having a good time and getting the attention of the staff (with perhaps a comment of praise now and then for exceptional performance). None of the children participating, however, get near the amount of individual attention from staff members or exercise as much control over staff behavior as the child that refuses to participate. Here we see that under standard child correction procedures it is the deviant behavior that pays-off. To gain special attention from the staff and exercise control over their behavior one does what is unexpected or unacceptable

23.   Under standard child correction procedures,

quite frequently it is _____

that pays-off.

---

22. attention   23. deviant behavior (inappropriate behavior)

In all these instances we see that the principles of behavior have 69 been misapplied. The result is that an inappropriate, unacceptable deviant behavioral response has been rewarded with special attention, while acceptable, appropriate behaviors go unattended. Disrupting other children while they are listening to a story pays-off (gets rewarded with attention) while sitting quietly and attentively does not (goes ignored). Hitting or attacking another child pays off (gets rewarded with attention) while being the victim does not (goes ignored). Refusing to participate in activities with other children pays off (gets rewarded with special attention) while being a regular participant does not. One may get some attention, but only as a part of a group, one is not singled out for *special considerations*.

> 24. Disrupting other children, hitting other children, refusing to participate in activities are behaviors that children use to _____ adults.

Examples Illustrating the Appropriate Approach To Appropriate Behaviors

The system, based on correct application of behavior principles outlined previously and presently being used by some treatment facilities for such children seeks to correct this "injustice" by giving rewards (tokens and praise) to children when behaving appropriately and ignoring children who behave inappropriately, thus also denying them tokens. In this way scientific principles of behavior are used to reward, and hence strengthen acceptable or appropriate behavioral responses. The child soon learns that appropriate behaviors pay-off (receive attention and exert control over the staff's behavior) and inappropriate behaviors do not pay-off (are ignored and exert no control over staff's behavior). This is the reverse of the approach to child training common in our culture.

> 25. Correct use of behavioral laws require that _____ behavior be rewarded and _____ behavior be ignored.

---

24. control

25. appropriate
inappropriate

26. This is frequently the _____ of present child training approaches in our culture.

As a result of our more precise understanding of the principles of behavior and how they operate to strengthen behavioral responses the three examples of inappropriate behavior presented above would now be handled differently.

Rewarding Attending Behavior

Under our new system the children who are attentively listening to the story would be given the complete attention of the staff. The aide reading the story would interrupt her reading from time to time to compliment the children on how well they are listening. At the same time she might give each of them a token. The children who are being disruptive would be ignored and would receive no tokens. Hence, their ability to participate in special events or use canteen and other privileges would be limited. They must learn to give up their deviant and disruptive behavior and participate with other children during such activities.

27. Proper use of behavioral principles requires that disruptive children be _____.

28. Children listening attentively to a story should periodically be _____.

Rewarding the Victim

Under this new program whenever one child aggresses toward another, staff members would ignore the aggressing child and give complete attention to the child who is being attacked. They might praise him for not striking the other child back and give him a token, all in full view of the aggressor. Children learn in this way that it does not pay to attack another child because he gets all the attention and earns the tokens while the aggressor goes ignored and tokenless.

---

26. reverse (opposite)   28. rewarded
27. ignored

29. Proper use of behavioral principles would indicate that when one child strikes another child the _____ child should get attention, not the _____.

Rewarding Cooperating Behavior

Recall an identical situation discussed in Chapter 4 (page 46). Here we cited an example of a child (Teddy) who was hitting his sister. The solution was to handle the problem by (1) ignoring the hitting behavior when it occurred and (2) establish situations where cooperative behavior toward sister could be rewarded. The approach given in the previous paragraph is another way to handle this problem. Whenever Teddy hits his sister, his mother could ignore him completely and give all of her attention and consideration to his sister. Hopefully, he would learn that hitting his sister does not pay-off. It succeeds only in earning her more attention and himself less. A combination of these approaches should be most effective.

Rewarding Participating Behavior

Finally, in this program, if a child refuses to participate in a group activity, he is ignored. No effort is made to get him to join the group. On the other hand, the activity is interrupted every ten to fifteen minute interval so that the staff can give tokens and praise to the participating children. Thus, the deviant non-participating behavior is no longer rewarded with special attention, while group participation is.

30. Children who refuse to participate in group activities when this is expected of them should be _____.

---

29. attacked   30. ignored
    aggressor

The approach toward correcting withdrawing behavior is not really as simple as just presented. Although the withdrawing child is ignored when not participating in large group events, special efforts must also be taken to train participating behaviors. In the case of the "acting-out" child, his behavior skills are often full and varied and many types of responses are being emitted. It is merely a matter of strengthening the more appropriate ones and eliminating the undesirable ones.

31. "Treating" the "acting-out" child is a matter of

_____ appropriate responses

and _____ undesirable responses.

In the case of the withdrawing child we are dealing with inactive and limited social skills. Many times there is an element of fear or insecurity present which is causing the child to inhibit his responding to the environment. We are confronted with the task of developing interacting skills where presently very little exists.

32. "Treating" the "withdrawing" child involves

_____ interacting skills.

The program set up to accomplish this task should make use of the principle of "shaping." The withdrawing child has to be retrained as one would a mentally retarded child (which we will discuss in the next chapter). His response range is limited and it needs to be increased. This can only be accomplished gradually in a step-wise manner following the techniques of shaping. One cannot simply put this type of child into a situation with other children to force interaction immediately. If the situation is not well-controlled and unpleasant consequences occur, the child may resist interactions still more. (If you are afraid to ride a bicycle and on your first attempt you fall down and skin your knee very seriously, you will be unlikely to make a second attempt.)

33. The "withdrawing" child must be _____

into interacting with other children.

---

31. strengthening   32. developing
    eliminating   33. shaped

In the first stages of the program the interaction attempted should be limited and controlled. If this child is being treated in an institution, the staff might begin by setting up situations where one staff member sits next to the child and converses with him. A second staff member can then reward the child for the interaction with the first staff member. Sitting close to another child at the dinner table can be arranged and any conversation between the two children should certainly be amply rewarded.

34. In the first stages of a program to increase the interaction of a child with other children or adults, the contacts should be _____ and _____.

Later, sitting next to another child in the play room can be an excuse to reward both of the children. When the other children begin to notice that they get rewarded whenever they're near a particular child, they will begin to spend more time near the child. This is one way to get the withdrawn child into a group—have the other children choose to be near him, rather than taking him into the group.

35. The slightest contact with another child should be _____ at the beginning of training.

Still later, tasks can be set-up where the withdrawing child is asked to assist one or two other children move a heavy object, for which they are all praised and rewarded. Short periods of participation in simple games (tossing a ball) involving two or three children can be rewarded. Gradually the time period, number of participants, and complexity of the interacting can be increased.

Such treatment programs (using tokens as rewards for appropriate behaviors) are quite flexible and can be fitted to the special needs of each child.* Within this over-all system special programs can be designed to deal with the specific behavioral problems or deficiencies of any child.

*Such programs, in actual practice, are much more complex. Only the basic theoretical skeleton of this general approach can be presented here. Nonetheless, it should by now have given you an appreciation for the general application of our new "science of behavior" to the correction of behavioral problems in children. See the references listed at the end of the book for more information on these systems.

---

34. limited
controlled

35. rewarded (attended to)

74 In this way the behaviors of all types of "problem" children may then become more acceptable to parental or societal wishes. This will result in more appreciation of the child by his parents, teachers, etc., and make life more pleasant and fulfilling than it may have been had he persisted in his maladjusted patterns.

When the Child Goes Home

If a child treated in this manner is sent back to his home where the same pay-offs are operating as they were prior to treatment (and which caused him to be placed there to begin with) then the success attained in treatment will be lost. If the child returns to a home where attention and praise are not given for appropriate responses they will soon begin to disappear. Similarly, if inappropriate behavior once again begins to pay-off, it will begin to occur more frequently. In a short while, the child will be right back to his old ways.

36. If the child is returned to a home where pay-

offs prior to treatment are still present, all gains

will be ——————————————————————.

If behavioral gains are to be maintained after the child is returned to the home, the family will have to reward the child for these behaviors in the same way the institution did. For this reason it is important for parents to know the laws of behavior and how to use them.

37. If behavioral gains are to be maintained, the

pay-offs in the home must be the —————————

as the pay-offs in the institution.

A few weeks before the child goes home, the parents will have to become involved in the child's treatment and learn the techniques of behavior change used by the treatment staff. In some cases, parents are involved in the treatment program throughout the child's stay at the institution so that even when he goes home on weekend visits the parents can continue to carry out the program.

38. Parents have to be involved in the child's

——————————————————————.

---

36. lost   37. same   38. treatment

Does this mean that the parents have to give tokens to the child when he comes home? In most cases no, due to the use of the principle of scheduling. Tokens are merely used at the beginning of the training procedures to strengthen the effect of social rewards (attention, praise). Once the child is "shaped up" (appropriate responses have been learned and inappropriate ones discarded) the staff can begin to gradually stop giving tokens and reward behavior with attention and verbal praise alone. At this point, many of the items and activities for which the child had to pay, now are available to him free. Often, the child is given a colored button to indicate that he has reached this level and this becomes a status symbol among the children. If he starts to use inappropriate behavior again, he loses his button and has to start all over earning tokens to pay for everything.

39. Once appropriate responses have been acquired

by the child the tokens can be _____.

At this point the parents can be brought into the training program (if they have not already been participating) and taught appropriate ways to give attention and praise for the child's behavior. Once the parents are trained in the correct use of this approach, the child can be discharged to the home.

40. The child should not be discharged home until

_____

_____.

Limit Testing

A common effect that occurs many times when we first begin to apply these behavioral laws to change behavior is what is called "limit testing." Many parents, no doubt, have had experiences with this effect, whether or not they realized what was happening. Limit testing is an attempt on the part of the child to see how far he can push the parents before they give in to his demands or punish him as they have done in the past.

---

9. gradually withdrawn   40 parents are trained in correct
                                     use of behavioral principles

41. Increasing one's behavior to force a pay-off from parents is called ―――――――――――――.

Many times, when a treatment program requires us to ignore a response which previously obtained attention and other pay-offs for the child, the behavior will actually increase in frequency before it decreases. Things may get worse before they get better. Because the original level of his response doesn't seem to pay-off any more (he is ignored) the child increases the intensity or frequency of the response hoping that this will force the parent to respond. This is similar to the adult who gets upset when a cigarette or candy machine doesn't work. He thinks that by pulling the handle a little harder or more frequently the cigarettes or candy may drop down. If he is unsuccessful, he soon gives up. So it is with the child. If he is unsuccessful, he soon gives up also and tries some other way to get his pay-offs.

42. If the original level of response no longer produces a pay-off the child is quite likely to ―――――――――――――the level of the response.

If one understands the principle of "shaping," one can see the terrible results of giving into the child when he starts to test limits. If a higher level of the response succeeds in getting the child what he wants, this level of the response is more likely to occur again. One has succeeded in rewarding and thus "shaping up" a worse response than the original one.

Therefore, once a decision is made to ignore a response, one must be prepared to tolerate an increase in its frequency before it begins to decrease. If the child's increased efforts do not panic the parents into giving up their "stoic inattentiveness," they will soon diminish.

43. If a child begins to increase the level of his responding in order to ―――――――――――――, the parent must ――――――――― this increase. Eventually it will decrease and disappear.

One way of weakening this effect is to set up a positive program of attending to and paying-off preferred behaviors at the same time one ignores unpleasant behaviors. In other words, one makes up for the loss of attention in one area by increasing attention in another area of behavior.

41. limit testing
42. increase

43. get a pay-off (get what he wants)
    ignore

44. Limit testing can be minimized by increasing

one's _____ for _____

behaviors.

Spoiling Children

Some parents have wondered if the token technique wouldn't lead to an extremely spoiled child—expecting pay-offs for everything he does.

First of all we must realize that there is nothing wrong with expect-nig pay-offs for our behavior. As a matter of fact, the whole point of the previous chapters was to show that the greatest majority of our behaviors are performed for that very reason—to get a pay-off. If the child was not interested in getting "things" as a result of his behaviors, he would become non-responsive and just vegetate.

45. Most behavior occurs in order to get _____.

The point we have tried to emphasize, however, is that the pay-off should come in the form of a social reward (attention, praise). Most children seek attention and recognition from their parents as reward for their behavior. There is nothing wrong with this. It is a positive "binding" relationship for the family unit. It increases the happiness, security and self-confidence of the child. It is the most positive and constructive way when used with the *withholding of social rewards* for inappropriate responses for shaping a child's behavior.

46. There is nothing wrong with a child seeking

_____ for his behavior.

A student in class was once asked, "What kinds of behavior do we associate with the so-called spoiled child?" With little hesitation she responded, "A child who expects everything for nothing." She was asked to rephrase her statement in the more scientific terms learned in the course. After a few moments of thought, she cautiously rephrased her response, "The spoiled child is one who expects *rewards* (pay-offs) that are *not dependent upon* his behavior." She earned an "A" in the course!

The spoiled child is one who has been raised on a schedule that gives him pay-offs without any regard to his behavior. His parents shower him with material and social rewards at any time without any consideration as to whether or not his previous behavior was appropriate or inappropriate. Rewards just come to him. He does nothing to earn them. He can even misbehave and still the pay-offs are there. This child grows up with the idea that good things belong to him just because he exists, not

---

44. pay-offs (attention)
preferred (appropriate) (desirable)

45. pay-offs (rewards)

46. rewards

because of how he behaves. He eventually expects this from everyone, not just his family. The world owes him not only a living but the best of everything.

47. A spoiled child's _____ are

_____ his

behavior.

If a child is raised in a manner indicated by our knowledge of behavioral principles, he will not behave as described above. Rather, such a child learns that rewards depend upon appropriate behavior. He comes to expect his pay-offs not because the world owes him a living, but to the extent that his responses earn them.

48. The child raised according to sound behavioral

principles learns that _____ are _____

appropriate behaviors.

Bribing Children

There is another type of child that is also the product of misapplication of behavior principles. This is the child that has been taught (quite accidentally, of course) that *good* pay-offs follow *inappropriate* behavior. This results from a common misuse of material rewards. Adults tend to use rewards to *bribe* the child into behaving correctly. "If you do so-and-so then I'll give you such-and-such a reward," is the common approach characteristic of the "bribe."

49. Learning that rewards depend upon inappro-

priate behavior occurs when parents _____

a child into behaving appropriately.

In setting up a token system in institutions, this is one of the first errors made by the treatment staff. It is also a common problem with parents who are attempting to use this method for correctly training their child. It is also the most difficult to overcome. But it must be overcome or one makes the child worse than better.

---

47. rewards   48. rewards   49. bribe
    not dependent upon   dependent upon

50. In setting up a token system in an institution

_____ is one of the first errors made

by the staff.

A token system was set up in an institution for treating disruptive children. One child was observed frequently to hit the other children. Following one of these outbursts a staff member went up to him, took his hand, led him to a chair, and said, "If you sit there quietly for five minutes, I'll give you a token." He sat quietly for five minutes, got his token, and shortly thereafter was back hitting the other children.

This child was accidently being taught that "if he hit another child someone would take him by the hand and lead him to a chair and then reward him with a token." He was learning that he had to misbehave before he would get a reward. You can be sure that in a short time the frequency of this type of behavior would sky-rocket.

51. The approach the staff member used in this

example was teaching the child that getting a

pay-off _____ hitting

other children.

Parents frequently bribe a child into being well-behaved although they don't always realize what they are doing. The child misbehaves and the parent says, "If you'll be good for the next fifteen minutes, I'll give you a cookie." Or, "If you stop fussing with your sister for the rest of the day, I'll take you both to the store for ice cream." The child misbehaves. This gets the parent's attention. He is then offered a pay-off for being well-behaved for a specified length of time. Once the pay-off is given, the child begins to misbehave again, so that another pay-off contract can be made. In this way the child increases his pay-offs.

52. Once the pay-off for a bribe has been given

the child _____ again in order to

be bribed again.

53. In this way the child _____ his

pay-offs.

---

50. bribing   52. misbehaves

51. depended upon   53. increases

A mother was going to the store to pick up a single grocery item. She wanted her daughter to wait in the car. The daughter wanted to accompany her mother so she began to make a fuss. The mother produced a package of gum and told her she could have a piece if she would "stay nicely in the car for mother." The child accepted the bribe. Although this approach permits the mother to cut short the problem and do her shopping, it also taught the child that making a fuss is rewarded with gum.

In using the laws of behavior one never bribes a child to "be good." Appropriate behaviors are rewarded only when they occur spontaneously or are developed through shaping. If a child is misbehaving, he should be ignored. However, at some later time when he is again behaving appropriately, he should at that time be rewarded. If it's candy or a token, also tell him why he is being rewarded ("You're reading"). If it's a social reward, you may simply say, "You're reading" or "That's an interesting story."

54. Appropriate behaviors should be rewarded only when they occur _____ or are developed by _____.

55. In using the laws of behavior one never _____ a child to "be good."

How To Express Praise or Approval

In rewarding a child with praise it is suggested that value-laden expressions of such praise be avoided. You ought not to say, "Jane is sitting, she's a *good* girl," "It makes mother *happy* to see Ted and Pam play together," or "Mommy *loves* you when you do that." When praising a child, the best rule of thumb seems to be to tell the child specifically why you are attending to or praising him. If Jane is sitting quietly, then draw attention to this behavior by merely saying, "Jane is sitting." The fact that you call attention to it is reward enough for Jane to continue to sit quietly. If Teddy and his sister, Pam, are playing nicely together, one might simply comment, "Teddy and Pam are playing together." A sincerely expressed "thank you" may be used to reward a job or favor after

---

54. spontaneously   55. bribes
    shaping

it has been completed. Calling attention to the quality of a job is im- portant, but the evaluation is directed toward the task, not the person. One can say, "That's a good job" but ought not to say, "you're a good boy for doing your job." In some cases, merely patting a child on the head or hugging him can be quite sufficient for rewarding the behavior. No words, other than a quick warm smile, need be exchanged. Immediacy of the reward will provide specificity.

56. When verbally praising a child the best rule

of thumb is to tell the child_____

why you are attending to or praising him.

57. At times a mere _____

or _____ can be a sufficient reward for

a behavior.

This type of approach rewards the behavior with attention and helps the child develop a positive regard toward himself based on his positive behaviors and by association, himself. Statements like "Mother loves you" or "Mother's so happy you are her little boy" may be best given when tucking the child in to bed at night and should not be specifically dependent on the child's behavior.

---

56. specifically

57. pat on head
    hug

Sharon Peters, Student Social Worker, Andrew McFarland Zone Center, Springfield, Illinois. Reprinted with permission of *Staff* published by the American Psychiatric Association.

Food is so often used as a reward in behavior-shaping that it came as a surprise to us to find that Mark, a shy, puny five-year-old boy who resisted all our attempts to interact with him, refused to eat solid foods.

He was an only child who had been overprotected by his parents after they learned he was retarded, and he had become a major behavior problem at home. He resisted toilet-training, had not learned to dress himself, and was rebellious and negativistic. Although his parents had been advised to withhold all food except solids, the mother could not bring herself to do so for long. She had soon reverted to blending his foods to the consistency of applesauce.

When Mark was brought to us, we considered placing him on our unit for retarded children, but his mother refused to be separated from him. We decided to let her undertake a behavior-shaping program at home. It seemed a good opportunity to assess the potential value of behavior therapy in a home setting, with the parents instead of the staff carrying out the training. I was to visit once a week to counsel and observe.

Before she began, the mother saw a movie, *Reinforcement Therapy*, produced by Smith Kline & French, which illustrates the basic principles of behavior therapy. She also observed the staff of our unit actually using the principles with the children. She was impressed at the value of verbal praise and immediate reward in helping severely retarded children behave more appropriately and she gained confidence in her ability to use the techniques with Mark.

In many behavior-modification programs, the children are given tokens for appropriate behavior. The tokens can be exchanged for a reward, usually food. In Mark's case, however, food would not work, so his mother decided to buy a selection of dime-store toys which he could obtain in exchange for tokens.

As in all behavior-shaping programs, the task (eating) was analyzed and broken down into successively more complicated parts, and Mark was required to succeed at only one part to get a reward. His mother was to feed him less blended food than usual so he would be moderately hungry, and then was to offer him a small piece of soft fruit or candy. At first she was to praise him and give him a token if he merely allowed her to place the food in his mouth, even if he spat it out again. She was cautioned not to coerce him and to make no fuss about his eating.

The next step was for Mark to swallow the piece of food, if he had not; for that he received another token. Next he had to eat larger portions and to accept soft vegetables. The blended formula was to be cut down as he accepted more solid food.

After only ten days, Mark was accepting solid food regularly, and only half his diet was blended. His parents were overjoyed, and the father, who originally had little confidence in the plan, now began to help with Mark's training. In another week, Mark was eating all solids except meat, and the blended formula was abandoned. His parents began to mix small pieces of meat with chili, spaghetti, and potatoes. A few days later, they offered Mark a small portion of hot dog, and he ate it.

The father, in his exuberance, began to offer Mark more and more meat, until the child began to resist again. We cautioned the father not to push too hard. The training progressed without problems until Mark was eating meat regularly.

In the beginning, the tokens purchased a small toy for Mark every night, but gradually the "price" was increased until he got one only every other night. His mother now is able to get the same results with verbal praise only. She is using the same methods to teach Mark to dress himself.

Mark's health has improved with the solid diet. He is beginning to recognize his own achievements and show pride in becoming independent. His parents have a much better and consistent relationship with him; they are able to be firm with him, and he knows what the limits are. For the first time, the three of them are going out together and doing things as a family.

When I go for my weekly visit, Mark waits at the window for me, and then shows me the toys he has earned since last week. He responds warmly to my praise. One day I surprised him with a bag of mint candies. He immediately started popping them into his mouth, and reacted gleefully to my pleasure.

6 The Retarded Child

When we speak of the retarded child, we are, of course, referring to a very broad range of mental and behavioral abilities. The two main divisions made among retardates are "educable" and "trainable." The educable retardates can attend special education classes where, with special attention and techniques, they can attain limited educational goals or accomplishments. The trainables are considered too damaged to be able to attain academic skills. They are, in fact, so limited that special attention in achieving even the most minimal personal and social skills is needed.

1. Severely retarded children need training in basic

_____

_____.

For the educable child, behavioral laws may be used in teaching educational skills as well as personal and social skills. For the trainable, behavioral laws are used mainly to shape social and self-help skills. These skills (dressing, feeding, toileting) need to be achieved before success in other areas can be acquired. Actually, training self-help skills is a basic necessity for all retardates. Because mothers are more concerned about and involved in teaching these skills, this chapter will be devoted to the use of behavioral laws in training the "trainable" retarded in such skills. If a mother is able to use these principles in this area of training, there should be little difficulty in applying them to other levels of retardates or other areas of training.

2. _____ are basic to

training in all areas among retardates.

_____

1. personal and social skills   2. self-help skills

At the present state of our knowledge the techniques and principles presented here are the only useful approaches for training retardates. In fact, these techniques are such an obvious procedure to use in training retardates, that it is difficult to understand why they were not used earlier.

Animal trainers have for centuries been training animals to perform in human-like ways by using behavioral laws. Yet retarded children have been denied these simple training techniques and permitted instead to idle like wild animals in institutions.

This is a puzzle. People resist the idea of using animal training techniques on retarded children, leaving them to live like animals, but spend much time in training animals to perform very human-like responses, even talking (parrots, myna birds). It is time to correct this injustice and use the principle of behavior training on these children so they begin behaving like the human beings they are!

3.   Training animals and training retarded children

require knowledge of the same basic _____.

Helen Keller's Story

The story of Helen Keller is an example. Before Miss Keller had a teacher she lived like an animal. For those of you who saw the movie or play "The Miracle Worker" you'll remember the pathetic scenes of her struggling about the table grabbing food off anyone's plate in order to eat. Her mother felt sorry for her, so little effort was made to train her in appropriate responses. This would have been too cruel, her mother reasoned.

When Helen's teacher, Ann, arrived, she corrected this situation (having been a partially sighted child herself) and forced Helen to behave like the human being she was. No more feeling sorry for this child and permitting her to live like an animal. A program of training was begun to assist Helen in developing her human abilities. Knock down, drag out battles ensued between Helen and Ann. They were hard on the conscience but very beneficial to Helen's development. Ann was anything but gentle and permissive with Helen. She knew that if Helen were ever to overcome her handicaps, she would have to learn to behave in a manner befitting a human being. To feel sorry for her, to do everything for her, to expect nothing from her because she was blind and deaf would result in a lifetime of subhuman behavior.

To gain the control over Helen's behavior that Ann needed she had the family remodel a small bungalow away from the main house where she and Helen could live by themselves. Here Ann had complete control

3. behavioral laws

over Helen's environment and, hence, over her rewards. She could de-87 termine if and when Helen received a "reward" for a particular behavior.

    4. Ann needed _____ over Helen's

       environment to be able to train her properly

       by determining if and when Helen received a

       _____.

Her basic reward was Helen's meals. Helen didn't eat until she learned table manners. If Helen grabbed food up in her hands, it was knocked out of her hands. She couldn't take a bite of food unless she used her spoon. If she refused to keep her napkin in her lap, the meal was removed and she went hungry. It didn't take Helen very long to develop proper eating behavior. So it went, Ann carefully observing Helen and directing her responses, rewarding Helen with food and affection when she responded appropriately, but withholding rewards when she failed to perform the proper response.

    5. Ann trained Helen through the use of _____

       for appropriate responses.

Due to Helen's sight and hearing handicaps it was especially difficult to communicate to Helen what was expected of her. Initially, the training sessions were quite strenuous on Ann, as Helen, (not understanding) resisted her efforts and tested limits. (Where the child's sight and hearing are intact and where behavioral principles are correctly used, the training sessions go very smoothly.) Had it not been for Ann and her intuitive awareness of the principles of behavior shaping, Helen Keller would have been lost to the world.

The story of Helen Keller illustrates the crippling effect of "feeling sorry" for handicapped children and the need to use the laws of behavior to direct these children to achieve the maximum of their abilities. Although such techniques have been applied to animal training and hence seem "inhuman" they are in fact essential for training retarded children to develop their full potential.

    6. Handicapped children can only be helped in over-

       coming their handicap through proper use of

       _____.

Learning Differences Among Children

All children learn. Some just learn more quickly than others. Why this is so, we cannot, with our present level of knowledge, be certain. It

---

4. control   5. rewards
   reward   6. behavioral laws

appears to be related to the ability of the central nervous system to handle the information relayed to it by the sense organs. Some can handle large amounts of information very rapidly. Others appear limited and need smaller units of information and slower rates of input. Retarded children appear to be handicapped in this way. Information for the retarded has to be broken down into small simple units which are presented slowly and repeatedly. When given these conditions the retarded child is capable of acquiring skills and knowledge far beyond what one might at first imagine.

7. Retarded children suffer central nervous system deficits which require that learning be broken down into _____ which are presented _____ and _____.

Reasonable Expectations for the Retarded Child

This is not to say that given the right training procedures a severely retarded child can learn to do multiplication and read books. It does mean, however, that given the right training procedure a severely retarded child can be trained to dress himself, feed himself and develop acceptable toilet habits. He can learn other manners that make him more presentable to the world in which he is living. With our present approaches such children are often put into institutions where their lives are so empty and repulsive that the public is generally not even permitted to tour the wards. Proper training techniques can help such children live up to their full potential even though that potential may not include "normal" abilities for understanding and responding. Whatever this potential may be (if it be only in expecting the child to take care of and respond to his basic bodily needs) one should always expect him to achieve this potential and never settle for less.

8. A severely retarded child may never read or do math adequately, but he can be required to achieve whatever _____ he has.

---

7. small units
   slowly
   repeatedly

8. potential

Proper use of behavioral laws do just this. The child is assisted in achieving his potential by (1) having a task or behavior broken down into small simple steps, (2) which are as distinct or clear as possible, and (3) presented in a repetitious, consistent manner. In addition, we make the child desire or want to learn this behavior by using rewards for success at each step of the way. In this way the child is encouraged to continue in his efforts.

> 9. A retarded child develops the desire to achieve
>
> his potential by being _____.

Structuring the Task for the Retarded Child

The "normal" child, for example, responds effortlessly to the procedures for dressing and picks up the social rewards (parental approval, smiles, etc.) for success in this area with little awareness. The severely retarded child is unable to respond to the usual procedure for dressing given by parents. He is unable to understand the parents' communication for this task and fails to learn to dress himself. As a result, he receives little or no social rewards for success in this area. But if the procedures are broken down into very clear and simple steps and if very specific rewards are given at very definite points along the way, the child will respond appropriately and learn to dress himself.

> 10. The reason the retarded child has difficulty in
>
> learning basic skills is due to his inability to
>
> _____.
>
> 11. In addition, failure in this area leads to few,
>
> if any, _____ for success.

It's not that the child can't learn to dress himself; it's that he can't learn to dress himself under the conditions by which parents naturally train such behaviors in their children. But if time and effort is taken to (1) break the behavior task down into simple parts, (2) present these parts systematically and slowly, and (3) very emphatically supply re-

---

9. rewarded for success at each step
   of the way

10. understand parent's communication

11. rewards

wards at the appropriate times then the severely retarded child can also learn to dress himself.

Attempting to teach a child to dress, eat, etc., in the usual way through verbal insistence, hasty demonstrations and punishment for failure often leads to negative feelings between mother and the child. If the mother insists that the child do something which he can't do (or fails when he attempts it) the child will soon resist the mother in all of her efforts to train him. The mother-child relationship is soon confronted with a succession of frustrations and failures and all interactions deteriorate.

12. Attempting to teach through verbal insistence and punishment for failure often leads to _____ feelings.

Teaching a Retarded Child To "Undress" and "Dress"

As an example of a training session making maximum use of behavioral principles, we have chosen to demonstrate a training procedure for undressing since it is one of the easiest behaviors to shape in the retarded child.

It is necessary to keep in mind that learning proceeds most easily when unnecessary parts of the procedure are eliminated. One of the basic rules in learning any behavior is the *order* in which the parts of the behavior are acquired. Varying the order introduces additional difficulties into learning the complete task. Another important rule of learning involves the *signal* given to get a response. Here also, additions to or variations in this signal disrupt the learning process.

13. In training a behavior in a retarded child, keep the order of presenting the parts of the responses and the signal for the response as _____ as possible.

---

12. negative   13. unvaried (unchanged) (consistent)

The first requirement is to reduce the undressing routine into small steps or units. This is simplified if the child is dressed with the same amount and type of clothing each day. The procedure requires the removing of the child's clothing in the following order:

1. Shirt (use knit pullover, wide neck)
2. Undershirt
3. Left shoe
4. Left sock
5. Right shoe
6. Right sock
7. Pants (use elastic waist shorts or jeans)
8. Underpants

The order stated above gives us eight sub-goals or eight tasks at the completion of which the child can be rewarded. The reward should consist of both praise and a small bit of the child's favorite food during the first part of the training program.

14. In training "undressing" there are eight tasks at

the _____ of which a reward

can be given.

During the first days of training each of the eight subgoals listed above must be broken down into smaller units or steps. The procedure might go as follows:

It is bedtime. Timmy is seated on the bed or chair facing you. He is fully dressed. You are wearing an apron with a plastic lined pocket containing eight bite-sized morsels of a favorite food (quartered sections of cookies which would have been part of his evening meal). You will also have an additional cookie to be given to him when he completes the entire task and is completely undressed—after step eight.

You begin by saying clearly and distinctly, "Timmy, it's time to take your clothes off." (It's useful to address the child by name before giving the command as this often gains his attention.) Timmy will not respond the first time because he does not understand what you are asking him to do. So you proceed to the first step of the task and say, "Timmy, take your shirt off." You may reach out and tug at it to call his attention to it. As you are tugging at the shirt you might even repeat the word, "shirt." Now grasp the hem of his shirt and pull it up over his head until his hands are freed and the neck band is at his forehead just above the

---

4. completion (end)

eyes. It is unpleasant to have the shirt dangling loose and the child will generally react spontaneously by attempting to pull it off the rest of the way. (If he doesn't, you can grasp his hands and direct them to the neck band and assist him in pulling it off.)

15. The first step in training the child to take off his

shirt is to pull it up over his head _____

_____

_____.

As he frees his head from the shirt, say, "Timmy took his shirt off!" Smile broadly, put one arm around his shoulders for a squeeze, and put a piece of cookie in his mouth with the other hand. You have just rewarded Timmy for taking off his shirt. Once he has learned the task of pulling the shirt off his forehead, the next step would be to remove his arms but leave the neck band at his neck and require him to pull the shirt up over his head. When he is performing this task easily, the third step may be to leave his neck and one arm in the shirt and require him to remove it from there. It is important that you require Timmy to *complete* the task to get the reward. That is to say, do not reward him unless and until the shirt is completely removed.

16. "Undressing" the child should not be

_____ until he has completely

_____ the article of clothing.

Before you know it, saying "Timmy, take off your shirt," will result in the entire chain of movements required to remove the shirt: from his being fully dressed to sitting there with his shirt in his hand eating a piece of cookie and smiling happily at you.

We have described only the procedure for removing the shirt. Each training session should include removal of all the clothes, in the same manner following the same principles. Each succeeding training session should result in greater and greater involvement of Timmy in the action, but, and this is very important, using the same amount *or less* of the physical rewards.

17. Each succeeding training session should require

greater _____ from the child but

the _____ or _____

amount of the physical rewards.

---

15. until his hands are free and the neck band is at his forehead, just above the eyes.

16. rewarded removed

17. involvement same less

When we started, we gave Timmy a quarter piece of cookie for each sub-goal he completed, plus one whole cookie when he was fully undressed. As training sessions progress, we give less pieces of cookie during training, saving them for the end. It will go something like this: "Timmy, it's time to take your clothes off."

1. "Timmy, take off your shirt."
   Timmy removes his shirt and opens his mouth for a piece of cookie, leaning against you for a hug.

2. "Timmy, take off your undershirt."
   Timmy removes undershirt and opens his mouth for a piece of cookie and his hug.

3. And so on through Step 8.

At this point, (after completion of Step 8) reward with the extra **cookie**. The first time you get all of these eight steps completed without having to assist him at all, Timmy is ready for the next phase in the undressing routine. He must now learn to run through two steps of the procedure instead of one in order to get a reward. We combine steps one and two—the shirt and undershirt routines—asking Timmy this way: "Timmy, take off your shirt; take off your undershirt." The latter should be spoken again just before he finishes removing his shirt, and repeated as, "Timmy, take off your undershirt" if he pauses after removing the shirt. Reward only after Steps 2, 4, 6 and 8, giving the rest of the reward after Step 8 as usual.

18. As the training proceeds, the child is required

    to do _____ before receiving a

    reward.

Later, rewards should be given only after Steps 4 and 8 and lastly only after Step 8. One can proceed as follows: "Timmy, it's time to take off your clothes." Pause and give him time to proceed unprompted at each step. Prompt with the command if necessary. Reward with your attention and smiles along the way. To train Timmy to accept delays in

---

18. more (more steps) (two steps)

reinforcement at the end of the routine, spend several seconds praising Timmy warmly after Step 8 before giving him his cookies. After several such sessions reduce Timmy's reward to just one cookie and eventually give this only occasionally (subprinciple of scheduling).

19. As the "undressing" routine is mastered by the child, the rewards can be _____.

Crying or tantrum behavior in any training session is best handled by turning away from the child and waiting patiently until he stops. If the behavior becomes too disruptive leave the room for five to ten minutes to let the child settle down more completely.

20. Disruptive behavior from the child is best handled by _____ him.

In the meantime, upon arising in the morning and from a nap, he will be taught to dress using the same principles. Start with the shirt pulled over his head and help him put his arm through the sleeve and pull it down over his abdomen. Later pull the shirt part way over his head and have him pull it down, and so on until he can put it on without assistance.

Teaching a Retarded Child To Feed Himself

Teaching the retarded child to feed himself proceeds along the same lines. The child is seated before a plate of food. The servings are not too large. Place a spoon in his hand (the one he uses to grasp food) and close your hand around his. Scoop up some food in the spoon and lift it to his mouth. Do this several times and then remove your hand from his just as the spoon touches his lips. After that, remove your hand a bit farther from his mouth, on each movement. The food is the reward, and the child will readily complete the movement of bringing the spoon to the mouth. Later, merely help him to scoop the food into the spoon. Let him raise it to his mouth by himself. Then teach him to fill the spoon. Soon you will merely need to supervise him. Praise and physical contact can also be used at appropriate times to reward the *completed* response (placing food in mouth). Any undesirable behavior here can be easily treated by removing the plate for a few minutes.

---

19. gradually reduced (phased out) 20. turning away from (ignoring)

21. Teaching a child to eat with a spoon requires correct use of the subprinciple of _____ that teaching dressing and undressing does.

22. Undesirable responses at the table can be handled by _____.

Teaching Toileting to the Retarded Child

In teaching the retarded child appropriate toilet behavior, a record of when and how often he wets or soils his clothes will assist in determining the proper times for placing the child on the toilet. A set time for placing the child on the toilet should be established. Arranging the rest of the child's schedule so that he does not have to be taken away from an activity he is enjoying to be placed on the toilet will facilitate success in this area. Some pleasant activity in the bathroom, unavailable elsewhere will also make the child more willing to be taken there. A floating toy in the sink or tub for the child to play with after he has used the toilet may serve such a purpose. Whenever the child is hungry, food or candy can be used as an immediate reward for voiding on the toilet.

23. Removing the child to the bathroom should not interrupt an activity the child is _____.

24. Going to the bathroom should be made as _____ as possible.

The use of definite verbal instructions are again stressed. The words you use to instruct him should be simple and repeated frequently. You may begin by saying, "John, come to the toilet." Take him by the hand and lead him to the bathroom, sit him on the toilet and place your hands on his knees and smile at him. "We'll play with the ducks in the water when you finish." Repeat several times very pleasantly what you want the child to do. "John, _____ in the toilet." If and when John goes, place the food reward in his mouth. Smile and say, "John used the toilet."

25. Instruction in any area of training should be _____ and _____.

---

21. shaping

22. removing the food

23. enjoying

24. pleasant (desirable)

25. simple
repeated frequently

When John begins to come willingly to the toilet and has begun to void there quite regularly the water play can be discontinued. A favorite snack or drink away from the bathroom after a good toilet response can be substituted and eventually this can be withdrawn as the smiles and approval of the parent keep John well rewarded for his efforts.

26. As the child comes willingly to the toilet and begins to void regularly, rewards can be given _____.

The next step is to get John to sit alone in the bathroom. This can be done gradually increasing the distance between you and John so that you need only accompany him to the bathroom door. (It is important that John be well-trained in dressing and undressing himself before this phase is begun so the need to lower and raise his pants does not add any frustration to the situation.) Hopefully, John will soon be going to the bathroom unaccompanied. Permitting the child to flush the commode can provide an additional reward for this behavior.

27. Children can be _____ into sitting alone on the toilet by _____ _____.

Pre-Toileting Training

For those children who have not learned toilet habits and who frequently wet or soil, a systematic plan to reward them for being dry and clean between trips to the toilet can be undertaken. Use an ordinary kitchen timer set to go off from five to forty-five minutes throughout the day. At the beginning of the day make up a random list of time intervals of between five and forty-five minutes. Set the timer to go off for the first interval (say fifteen minutes). When the signal is heard, shut off the timer and reset it for the next time interval (perhaps, this time for thirty-five minutes). After you have done this, check the child to see if he is dry and clean. If he is found to be dry, reward him appropriately. (Lots of

26. away from the bathroom

27. shaped
   gradually increasing the distance
   between you and him

physical attention, approval and a favorite food.) If he is wet, say nothing, leave the child immediately, turning your back to him. Return a few minutes later (five to ten minutes), take him to wherever it is necessary to change him. While changing him say little or nothing and remain non-committal. Change him quickly and leave him or return him quickly to wherever you want him. The important thing is not to attach any social rewards to this procedure. The child, unless severely retarded, should soon learn the connection between being dry and obtaining rewards and being soiled and therefore ignored. Of course, it is important that the child be placed on the toilet at regular intervals during this training.

28. Children who soil themselves frequently can be trained to _____ the frequency of this response by being checked at various intervals of from five to forty-five minutes throughout the day and _____ if they are found to be dry and clean.

29. When changing a child who has soiled his pants, be sure to keep the _____ to a minimum.

Assessing Physical Readiness

In dealing with the severely retarded child (or any child for that matter) one must always be certain that the child is physically developed to the point where he can perform the response if given the proper training. A child cannot be expected to learn bowel habits, for example, if the retention muscles are not developed enough to be under voluntary control. For this reason, it is essential that the child be thoroughly evaluated as to his physical capabilities for performing the response. One must also be certain that other skills related to the response are also trained, as for example being able to dress and undress so he can raise and lower his pants.

---

28. decrease (reduce)
    rewarded

29. social rewards (attention)

30. Before training a child, one should be certain

that his _____

and other _____ are sufficient

for performing the task.

Lastly, the guidelines given here are presented merely to suggest types of approaches that are consistent with the correct application of behavior principles. There are, no doubt, other ways in which these and other problems of the retarded child can be handled. The important consideration is to understand and correctly apply sound behavioral principles. The creativeness with which one approaches the task in terms of developing routines, providing rewards, etc., is then a matter of individual choice.

Lori Learns to Walk

John S. Lowe, Child-Care Worker, Stephen Douglas Hall, Andrew McFarland Zone Center, Springfield, Illinois. Reprinted with permission of *Staff*, a journal of the American Psychiatric Association.

Lori, a six-year-old blonde, was the first child admitted to Stephen Douglas Hall, a residential treatment center for severely retarded children. She was microcephalic. The mid-line of her skull had hardened too quickly and prevented normal development of her brain. She was also afflicted with cerebral palsy and had never walked. But she adapted well to the unit and quickly attached herself to the staff members assigned to her. Her blue eyes would beam with recognition as she scuttled across the floor to us on her knees, her arms raised for us to lift her up and hug her.

Her knees and shinbones were covered with coarse calluses, her leg muscle somewhat atrophied, and her feet slightly deformed. She spent most of the time sitting on the floor, her legs tucked under her buttocks. She could stand if supported by another person, but disliked being made to do so, and she would usually cry and struggle when we tried to make her stand.

30. physical capabilities
skills

Lori's parents had taken her to many professional people and agencies. With her multiple handicaps, there was little hope that she could ever walk. Now she could easily be carried around, but as she grew older and heavier, the burden on her overtaxed parents would be even greater. A life-long stay in an institution seemed inevitable, but her parents resisted such a sentence. If only she could learn to walk, they pleaded, she might learn other basic skills, such as feeding herself, dressing, and going to the toilet.

Because we had failed to teach her to walk by direct attempts we decided to try methods developed by behavior-modification specialists. We chose two principles. The first was shaping, which means that the various parts of a task are broken down into successive steps, beginning with the simplest and working up to the completed task. As the individual masters each step, he is encouraged and is eventually able to complete the desired task.

The other principle, reinforcement, is based on the fact that people tend to repeat actions that lead to pleasant outcomes and abandon those that have unhappy results. Thus staff members were to reward Lori with attention, praise, and tidbits whenever she tried to stand or walk, and ignore her when she was sitting on the floor. While she was sitting on the floor, she would have no toys and would be kept away from other children. If she had to be carried somewhere, the staff member was to pick her up and move her quickly without speaking to her or smiling at her.

The important thing was to make Lori want to walk. She had to learn that being down on her knees was the coldest, loneliest feeling in the world and that standing up was wonderful and exciting because people did nice things for her. She did not understand language, so these things could be communicated only by the way we behaved.

It was terrible for us all when Lori recognized us as we came on duty and scuttled over on her knees for her expected hug and kiss. We had to look away and walk past her, ignoring the tiny tear showing on her cheek. But the training worked well, and when I arrived one day, Lori was waiting for me at the door, standing up. She had pulled herself up by the crossbar on the door and was holding on. I swept her up in my arms and lavished praise on her.

In the early days, Lori was rewarded for anything barely resembling an attempt to arise from the floor. As her training went on, rewards became harder to get. She had to pull herself up by a chair to get attention. To accelerate training, she literally walked for all her meals. A set of parallel bars was installed in a training room, and Lori spent mealtimes walking from one end of the bars to the other for a spoonful of her favorite food. If she refused to walk and sat on the floor, she went hungry until the next meal.

Soon she was walking with help and was given more freedom of movement. She loved to go outside and was allowed to stay out as long as she continued to walk or stand up. If she sat on the ground, she was brought back to the unit and left alone for fifteen or twenty minutes.

After about five weeks, Lori was discharged to go with her parents to Colorado. Her training was not finished, but she had learned to walk with a little assistance, usually just by holding on to somebody's finger. Her mother had spent the last week with us, learning the techniques the staff used in Lori's training so she could continue the program at home.

A few weeks earlier, she had wept at the thought of placing her daughter in an institution for the rest of her life. Now there was some hope. Lori had a long journey to make, but she would be able to make it with her family.

Using behavior principles in training appropriate behaviors in children is effective because (1) young children respond readily to such basic rewards as candy or gold stars which can be exchanged for toys and (2) they are almost completely dependent upon their parents or attending adults for such social rewards as praise or a reassuring smile.

The Social Value of Peers

As the child enters the adolescent stage, this situation changes. It takes more than candy and gold stars to satisfy an adolescent. Social rewards from parents, while valued, are less desired than social rewards from the other persons of his age group with whom he associates or perhaps another adult. An adolescent's behavior is most often directed toward increasing or maximizing social attention and approval from his peers, rather than from his parents.

1. It becomes more difficult to influence the behavior

    of children as they grow older because they seek

    rewards from _____ rather than

    _____.

Why Parents Fail

Many parents fail to realize this and become upset when they find their influence on the adolescent weakening. In desperation, parents may

1. peers
   parents

102 resort to punishment or threats of punishment to keep the child in line. This generally serves merely to drive the adolescent further away and weaken their influence even more. Other parents attempt to keep their adolescents in line by haphazardly increasing rewards. These may take the form of praise and approval applied indiscriminately, large allowances, special privileges or access to cars and liquor. When this fails, these children are referred to as "ungrateful" or may even be considered selfish and/or demanding. Of course, the fact that parents increase the punishment or use bribery to bring him in line indicates that they probably relied on these tactics in the past to control the child and this implies incomplete awareness of behavioral principles. Having used them incorrectly when the child was growing up, they can hardly expect to properly direct the behavior of an adolescent seeking to assert his independence from the home.

2. When parents begin to lose control over their adolescent, they may respond by resorting to _____ or _____ to regain their control.

Possible Outcomes of Inappropriate Behavioral Approaches

Improper use of behavior principles could follow several courses. The three most common tend to be (1) stressing negative pay-offs (punishment), (2) pay-offs given that are not dependent upon appropriate behaviors ("spoiling"), or (3) very few pay-offs being given at all (ignoring).

Home situations where punishment has been used to keep the child in line may result in an insecure, fearful child whose behavioral responses have been so inhibited that he has few behavioral abilities as an adolescent. As a result, he may become a withdrawing or non-participating child. Another outcome is that as he grows independent of the home, he may so resent his parents' treatment of him that he turns completely away from their influence. If on the other hand his inappropriate or deviant responses were the only means of obtaining adult recognition as a child he may carry these learned inappropriate behavior patterns right on into adolescence. Similar results may develop from the child being ignored. In the home he may have had little chance to obtain parental attention even by behaving inappropriately. Once he achieves the freedom from the home that adolescence gives him, he may find ways to engage in anti-social behaviors outside the home (for example,

2. punishment
bribery

reaking the law) that force his parents' or the community's attention. 103 n the case of the "spoiled" child, the outcome is obvious. He enters dolescence with the idea that rewards should come his way regardless f what he does. He may even discover that one way to increase one's ay-offs is to engage in inappropriate behavior thereby getting his arents to promise him more rewards if he behaves according to their ishes or desires.

3. Anti-social behavior outside the home may be a

   way of obtaining _____

   on the part of the adolescent.

Choosing Friends

As mentioned previously, the pay-offs applied by the friends with which the adolscent spends his time are now of primary importance. 'or the majority of adolescents, the behaviors that occur are influenced nore by what his peers are doing or what they expect than by parental ishes. Which simply means that, if parents want to be reasonably sure n adolescent behaves according to their standards, they must insure that e establishes a group of friends whose behavioral patterns are aceptable to them. In this manner, the behavior desired by the parents will lso be rewarded by the peers.

4. If parents want to insure that an adolescent be-

   haves according to their standards, they must

   insure that he establishes a group of friends whose

   behavior patterns are _____

   to them.

Determining Appropriate and Inappropriate Behaviors

What is meant by appropriate or inappropriate behaviors needs ome consideration and careful thought on the part of the parents. With dolescents, this is not a simple issue. For one thing, there is a possibility f disagreement between what parents consider appropriate and inppropriate behaviors and what the adolescent and his friends consider ppropriate or inappropriate. If parental expectations for the adolescent's

---

parental attention   4. acceptable

104 behavior are very much different from what his peers accept or deman as appropriate, the chances of getting the adolescent to meet thes expectations are greatly reduced. There may even result a complete los of influence over the adolescent as the parents come to be seen a "squares."

There are no absolute rules by which to settle this problem. Parent have a right and responsibility to set up limits and expectations for a adolescent's behavior. On the other hand, their limits and expectation should be realistic and determined to some extent by what adolescent in general are doing. Perhaps at this point we can only call to parent attention the need to be reasonable and realistic in what they expec of an adolescent.

5. If parental expectations are in conflict with that

of peers, the adolescent is more likely to conform

to his _____ expectations.

Even when the parents' expectations are most reasonable, situ ations develop where an adolescent is relating to a group of friends whic encourage and reward deviant behaviors. Such situations become eve more difficult for the parents to correct when "upsetting one's parents" o "getting the ole' man's goat" is itself rewarded by the group th adolescent runs around with. The degree to which one out-smarts o ignores one's parents is often a status symbol for gaining group approva When this attitude is extended to *all* adults, serious problems develop which may end in conflicts with the law.

If the parent-adolescent relationship has reached a stage wher disagreements concerning appropriate behaviors have become a constan source of friction in the home, there are some suggested steps which ca be followed in attempting to correct the situation.

Steps To Follow in Making Changes

In assisting parents to reassert their influence over their adolescent' behavior, one first has to get a commitment from them to apply positiv behavioral principles to the situation; namely, to reward appropriat behaviors and withhold the rewards from inappropriate responses. Onc a commitment to follow a positive approach has been made, the followin, steps should be considered.

Analyze the Situation

(1) Analyze the situation to determine exactly what behaviors ar

---

5. peers' (friends')

upsetting or displeasing. Be specific. Such vague statements as 105 "he's disrespectful" or "she doesn't mind" are not very helpful. The actual behaviors have to be pinpointed. "He curses his mother whenever she corrects him." "He ignores requests that he clean up his room or cut the grass." "She stays out every night of the week till 1:00 or 2:00 in the morning without telling anyone where she is."

> 6. In correcting a behavioral problem one needs to
>
> be _____ about the upsetting or
>
> displeasing behavior.

Determine Consequences

(2) What were the consequences to the adolescent of past behavior? Indicate how such situations have been handled in the past. Have you been relying too much on negative consequences? How have you been rewarding appropriate behaviors? Have you arranged any consequences at all?

Indicate Desired Behavior

(3) Indicate what you would like to see him/her doing. The best way to proceed is to list specific behaviors the adolescent is doing that you want to see eliminated or reduced. Then make a list of desirable behaviors that you want increased.

Conflicting With Peers

(4) Determine if these requests conflict with what his friends are doing. Is what you are expecting of this adolescent so out of line with what his friends are doing that to follow your wishes he receives the disapproval of his friends? If so, it will be very difficult to change these behaviors. The parent will have to use a very creative approach or supply very powerful rewards.

> 7. If the parents' expectations for an adolescent
>
> _____ with what his friends are
>
> doing, it will be difficult to change his behavior.

Compromising

(5) If at all possible, parents should try to establish a compromise between their expectations for the adolescent and what his friends are doing. It is important to evaluate your expectations against the

---

6. specific   7. conflict (differ)

need of the adolescent to move away from the home to an independent existence on his own in the world. In getting along well in later life he will generally have to get along with people his own age, not people his parents' age.

Rather than require him to give up some behavior completely, it might be better to let him continue the behavior but within the limits you can accept. There are, of course, behaviors for which parents can't compromise (like stealing hubcaps from cars). Here the parents have to really be creative in establishing pay-offs to make such behaviors less desirable to the child. The fact that punishment or threat of punishment from the law does not usually succeed in eliminating this behavior in so-called adolescent delinquents should clue parents in on the uselessness of this approach.

At some point, you have to sit down with the adolescent and discuss the situation with him. Find out from him what he considers reasonable expectations for his behavior. Avoid always dictating to him. Try to get him to make suggestions.

8. Parents may have to _____

on the behavioral expectations they have for an

adolescent.

Involving the Adolescent

(6) It is especially important to seek from him his opinions on what he considers to be acceptable rewards for performing appropriate behaviors. The adolescent must be involved in deciding what the pay-offs will be and how and when they will be given. There is no need to be secretive.

Many people feel that behavior principles have to be used without the individual being aware of what is happening. They believe that if he knows what's going on (that he's being shaped into behaving in a certain manner) he will not go along with it. When an individual reaches the age where he can understand these principles, to manipulate him without his awareness is a questionable practice. The secrecy of their application should not be a factor in their effectiveness. Knowing we are being rewarded for our appropriate responses in no way reduces the value of the reward.

---

8. compromise

9. Behavioral principles work effectively regardless of whether or not the person is _____ of them.

10. Adolescents should be involved in deciding what the _____ will be for their behavior.

Expectations and Pay-Offs

(7) The parent and adolescent now set up a list of responses they expect from *each other*. If the adolescent does such-and-such, the parent will supply such-and-such a pay-off. If the parent does such-and-such, the adolescent will supply such-and-such a pay-off. A relationship based on mutually agreed upon behaviors and mutually agreed upon pay-offs is established.

The following situation shows how a divorced mother and her son were assisted in setting up such a mutually agreed upon program to bring better relations into a home life that had deteriorated into a process of constant bickering, punishment, and disrespect.

Brian: A Problem in Disobeying

Brian was causing his mother much concern. He could be found at the pool hall almost every night of the week. She didn't mind this but many of the other adolescents that frequented the pool hall had been in trouble with the law and they had a strong influence on Brian's behavior. He had already been in trouble with the police for stealing a car. He and several other boys had found an unlocked car one night, crawled in and drove it around for the rest of the evening, intending to abandon it when it ran out of gas. He had been paroled to the custody of his mother but she could no longer control his behavior.

In spite of her persistent threats of locking him in his room or calling the police, he continued to leave the home every evening and stay away till all hours of the morning. Because he had been a problem in school, he had been dismissed for several days so he had even less reason to be home early. Some nights he would not come home at all. He remained away from home two or three days in a row with his mother not having the slightest idea where he was. When Brian returned, he gave her no explanation at all.

---

9. aware   10. pay-offs (rewards)

Brian's mother was not the only one having this type of problem. Other parents, when she called asking about Brian, also indicated that their sons or daughters were unaccounted for. Some parents were concerned. Others appeared not to be concerned at all. One day she had, in complete desperation and frustration, attempted to beat him with a lamp cord. Brian dashed into the kitchen and placed a knife on his wrist, threatening to kill himself if she didn't leave him alone. She called his bluff and he cut his wrist. It was, however, far from the vein and amounted to little more than a scratch. At this point, the mother went for professional help.

11. In her frustration, Brian's mother got caught in the error of thinking that _____ would stop Brian's inappropriate behaviors.

Two things were obvious: (1) Brian's friends were a strong influence on his behavior, (2) the mother had become trapped in using punishment or threats of punishment in her attempts to end his unacceptable behaviors. She was also very inconsistent in applying it.

It was obvious also that the mother could not completely prevent Brian from associating with his friends at the pool hall. It was also evident that these friends stayed out most of the night and often on weekends, not coming home at all for two or three days. It was, therefore, unlikely Brian could be made to give up this behavior, at least, not right away.

The mother was led to see that she first of all had to reestablish her influence over Brian by approaching him in a positive way. She had to pay-off with rewards rather than threats and punishment. She had been providing Brian with an allowance every week which she generally gave to him regardless of his behavior. Sometimes when she was especially upset, she'd withhold it for a while or only give him part of it.

In talking with Brian, one thing that "bugged" him about his mother was that she talked too much. She was always questioning him about everything. According to him, "she never had her mouth shut." In addition, she did not respect the privacy of his room. She was always coming in to "bug" him with her talk or to snoop.

The Plan

After much discussion, a program attempting to correct the faulty behavior principles being used in this situation was set up. The following expectations and pay-offs were mutually agreed upon.

---

11. punishment

Brian's mother wanted him to be home every week night by 11:00 P. M. He could stay out an hour later if he called her by eleven to let her know he would be home by 12:00. On Friday and Saturday nights he could stay out till 1:00. He could in fact stay out all night if he called her before 12:00 and notified her where he was and with whom he would be staying and assured her that an adult was present. If he stayed out all night, he was to call in the next morning before noon to let her know how he was.

Brian's mother wanted some other things from him also but was cautioned to begin with only this limited step. She had to first determine if she could reassert some influence over Brian. He needed time to adjust to this new approach. If the program worked out and Brian responded appropriately, other behaviors could be shaped later.

Brian wanted his mother to (1) not come into his room unless she had his permission. If a "do not disturb" sign was on his door, she was not to bother him. (2) If his mother began to "bug" him with too much talk, he was to request a "time-out" period and she was to not say another word to him for fifteen minutes.

Brian was not to receive a regular allowance at the end of the week, but his allowance would be accumulated daily depending upon his fulfilling the previous expectations. Every night he was home by 11:00 P.M. he received one dollar or if he called in and got home by 12:00 he still got the dollar. If he got home by 12:00 but failed to call in, he lost fifty cents. For each hour out past 12:00 he lost one dollar. If he stayed out on a Friday or Saturday night without calling in, he lost his allowance for that day and so forth. Each violation of an expectation clearly spelled out its effect on his allowance. On the other hand for each half hour he spent studying in his room before 9:00 he received fifty cents to two dollars maximum. He received fifty cents for each hour he was home between 9:00 and 11:00. In this way, Brian would earn as much as twenty-one dollars a week in allowance. With this he was to take care of all his expenses including buying clothes, buying food at school, etc.

If the mother followed her rules, Brian did not have to reward her. If she violated any rule (either talked after he called for "Time-out" or entered his room without his permission), he could add an hour onto his stay-out schedule or get fifty cents added to his allowance.

The reader may, at this point, question why the mother should be on a negative pay-off system. She gets punished, so to speak, by having to make concessions to Brian when she violates her rules. Brian doesn't reward her if she fulfills her contract. This is contrary to the emphasis placed on the value of a positive approach. If Brian can expect pay-offs for his appropriate behaviors from his mother why shouldn't she expect the same from him. Two considerations resulted in deciding to use this approach. (1) Since the mother-son relationship had broken down and Brian showed the most resistance to changing his behavior, it was decided to begin with a schedule which emphasized his pay-offs. (2) It was felt that the therapist would be the rewarding agent for the mother. The therapist would call her every other day to see how the program was working and compliment her if she upheld her end of the contract. Hopefully, once the mother-son relationship got on a more positive footing Brian would become a positive pay-off agent for his mother.

The plan was discussed with both individuals and the expectations and pay-offs agreed upon by both. In this way both mother and son felt they had influence over the other's behavior, knew clearly what was expected and knew what the consequences were for violating the expectations.

12. Both mother and son, at this point, decided upon

   mutually acceptable _____

   and _____ for changing each

   other's behavior.

In approaching an adolescent in this way, we don't expect to change too many behaviors all at once. Start with one problem behavior. After having corrected it to your satisfaction, move to another. Even with adolescents, "shaping" behavior gradually is the best way to proceed. If you expect changes in too many areas at once, the result can be frustration for both you and the adolescent.

Brian's mother didn't expect too much change at once. If she had insisted that Brian never go out on week-nights or never stay out over-night on weekends (something all his friends were doing), he probably would not have accepted the program. Once she gains some control over his behavior and a positive relationship begins to develop between them, additional "bargains" can be undertaken later. Brian's mother was also encouraged to talk with some of the other parents to see if they might not use a similar program with their children. In this way, the group pressure to stay out all night would also be weakened.

13. Brian's mother dealt with one problem behavior

   at a time to take full advantage of the principle

   of _____.

If the reader will look back over the preceding chapters, it will be

_____

12. expectations (behavior)   13. shaping
    pay-offs (rewards)

noted that control over one's own children must be bought at what may be a very dear price to some of us. It requires that we study our child and his friends as well as our own responses. Most of all perhaps it requires that the parent attend to the child—really see him, hear him and know him. Only in this way can the first steps be taken toward a constructive relationship.

Playing "Respond Appropriately"

This case history taken from: Patterson, Gerald; Ray, Roberta; Shaw, David; "Direct Intervention in Families of Deviant Children"; *Oregon Research Institute;* Vol. 8; No. 9; December, 1968. (Slight changes or modifications have been made in the text of this case history so that it would be easily understandable to the audience to whom this manual is directed, persons with no previous background in scientific behavior theory.)

"John was a four-year-old boy referred by the Child Welfare Department because his mother could not control his behavior. He had three or four temper tantrums each day. He was described as being generally very hyperactive, negativistic and was thought to be mildly retarded. Frequent spankings had not been effective. Recently he had begun to steal candy and trinkets from stores."

"The family consisted of a six-year-old brother, a three-year-old sister and the mother. Mother and father were separated. The family was now supported by the Aid to Dependent Children Program. The mother was twenty-three years of age, and had a tenth grade education. She was distraught over John's behavior and eager to see some changes made."

Following the baseline observation in the home, the psychologist "reviewed with her the problem behaviors which she wished to see changed. She listed John's extreme negativism, temper tantrums and hitting as being her primary concerns. She also said she would like to change his getting up early in the morning while the rest of the family was asleep and creating chaos in her kitchen. He would empty out the drawers, take food, and make messes on the floor."

"In the first session a series of situations were created in which the social worker made requests of John. For example, she would ask, 'Please pick up that magazine over there and bring it to me.' As John looked toward the magazine, she responded, 'Good, he is going to help me,' and dropped an M & M candy into a dish. 'He has already earned one M & M. Let's see how many more he can earn.' As John walked across the room, the psychologist continued to support his behavior with both verbal and candy rewards. As John returned with the magazine, the rest of the family 'cheered him on.' The whole family then took turns in suggesting requests which he could and did follow."

"The first forty-minutes practice session was planned as if it were a game and at the end the candies earned were shared with all the children. The mother was instructed to conduct similar sessions throughout the day. During the mother's sessions John earned points that could be used to purchase trinkets and toys for all the children from a supply which the psychologist had available. If John failed to follow a request or refused, he was simply ignored."

"Situations were also created in which John was to play with his brothers and sisters. He was rewarded for appropriate behaviors during these sessions with, 'That's very good; you have been playing now for several minutes and you have not been fighting. That is worth a point.' The mother was also to note any situation during the day in which John played with his brother and sister without fighting. This also earned John points."

"The psychologist returned the next day and dispensed the rewards earned by John during the previous twenty-four hours. The mother indicated that the practice sessions had gone very well and there had been almost no fighting or resistance. The other children were delighted with the toys earned by John's efforts."

A program was then started to keep John from getting out of bed in the morning before other family members and messing the kitchen. "John was given an electric clock which was placed by his bed. When he awoke in the morning he would start the clock and for each two minutes that he remained in bed he would earn an M & M. He was told that if he 'cheated' he would lose points." He slept in the mother's bedroom for a few days so that she could supervise this procedure until John could reliably do it himself.

"On the occasion of each visit the psychologist continued to practice the instruction following non-fighting interactions and discussed any problems which the mother might have had in her practice sessions during the day."

"During the third and fourth sessions one further training procedure was introduced. The mother's 'no' had little control over John's behavior. The mother had seldom provided any clear-cut consequences for John's either following or not following a command. The psychologist arranged a series of practice sessions in which John was reinforced for responding to a firm 'No.' For example, as John walked toward the door, the psychologist said, 'No, John, you cannot go outside.' As John turned around, she followed with, 'Very good, that is certainly worth a point.' Several dozen such trials were carried out each day by both her and the mother."

"After a series of four training sessions, the mother reported marked changes in John's behavior. As she continued to supply positive rewards for appropriate behaviors, she became increasingly effective in influencing his behavior. One month later, she reported few temper tantrums and no instances of stealing or early morning assaults on the kitchen."

8 ADULTS

The use of behavioral laws for improving the lives of adult human beings is finding application in many areas. The most exciting application is in treating persons who have spent many years of their lives in mental institutions. With the correct use of these principles, bizarre behavior patterns which have persisted for years are now being completely eliminated. Patients who had been thought "incurably ill" are being discharged from mental hospitals with no signs of ever having been a mental patient.

Rewarding "Normal" Behavior

The principles used are the same as outlined in previous chapters. Using the "law of reinforcement" as the basic "tool," the few signs of "normality" found in these disturbed patients are encouraged with attention, praise, and physical rewards. As these "normal" or appropriate behaviors are rewarded, they usually begin to increase in frequency. As the frequency of appropriate behaviors increases, still more rewards are given for such behaviors and so on until a positive cycle of appropriate behaviors and rewards for these behaviors are established.

  1. A reward is an event which ———————————

      the frequency of a behavior that it follows.

Previously, these patients were given up as hopelessly disturbed and left to live out the remainder of their lives in the back wards of the mental hospital being ignored for most of their days. Attention was

---

1. increases

114 given to them only when their disturbed behavior threatened to upset the ward routine, other patients, or harm the patient himself. Otherwise they became a part of an anonymous mass left to vegetate away the rest of their lives. The mental hospital staff responded to the inappropriate behaviors of these adults just as the inappropriate behaviors of children were attended to as discussed in Chapter 5. In the hospital the doctor spent more time going over their abnormal behavior in order to understand what it symbolized than attending to the few appropriate behaviors that the patient still performed. The early approach to severe mental problems always saw the bizarre behavior of the mentally ill as a symbolic expression of an unconscious conflict in the "personality." In fact, because of the shortage of doctors in such institutions, it was often impossible for a patient to see him unless he had been especially disturbed or upset or was acting bizarrely. Whenever a patient was being presented for observation and discussion before a group of visitors or panel of doctors, the patient with the strangest, most unusual behavior was selected for this presentation. You should by now see how this served many times to reward and thereby increase the frequency of these bizarre or strange behaviors. The patient became a special case, received attention and became important to the extent to which their abnormal responses amazed or baffled the staff.

2. _____ was earned by only the most unusual behaviors.

A Study in Correcting Eating Behavior

Ben spent many years starting and ending his day standing in a corner staring at the wall. He had spoken few words to anyone. The only time he left his corner was when he was taken hand-in-hand by a young student nurse and led to the dining room for his meals. He was also assisted in feeding himself by this attractive young girl who talked reassuringly to him throughout the meal.

3. The staff had probably rewarded Ben's behavior of standing and staring at the wall by an occasional kind word as they saw him in his familiar spot, thereby gradually _____ up this response.

4. Ben seldom spoke because his remarks were not given _____ or if attended to were never acted upon.

2. attention   3. shaping   4. attention

One day the staff of this hospital realized that they were guilty of misusing behavior laws. Attention and concern was being given to patients for their inappropriate behaviors rather than their appropriate behaviors. It was thereupon decided that no patient was to be led to his meals. Instead, a bell was to be sounded and the patients would be given ten minutes to get to the dining room. If they did not go to the dining room by the allotted time, they simply missed a meal. No fuss was to be made over them.

The first time this was done, Ben stood by the wall. As the meal time passed and no one had led him to the dining room, a few signs of distress (shuffling his feet, turning his head) appeared. He remained at the spot and went hungry. The same thing occurred for the evening meal and he went to bed not having eaten since breakfast. The next morning he was again left to stand in the hallway rather than being led to breakfast. Everyone else was at breakfast. He stood alone and deserted in the hallway outside his room. After several minutes, he began to shuffle towards the nursing station down the hall. He stood in the doorway but said nothing to the nurse on duty. She continued with her work as if he weren't present. Breakfast was over and he continued to be ignored. He did, however, remain in the area of the nursing station rather than return to his wall. Lunch came and the bell rang for all to go to lunch. Again this patient was deserted, except for the nurse at the desk. A few minutes later he appeared at the door of the nursing station. He looked distressed. The nurse continued about her work. Suddenly he spoke. His words were broken but clear, "Nobody has taken me to eat for two days!" The nurse turned to him very matter-of-factly, pointed to the dining room and said "There's the dining room. If you're hungry, go in and eat." After a few moments hesitation, Ben shuffled off to the dining room. As he came out of the cafeteria line with his tray of food, the pleasant young nurse who had previously led him to his meals approached him, flashed a warm smile, and affectionately led him to his table. He was soon on his way to recovery. The staff had simply decided that Ben's inappropriate behaviors were being rewarded by attention and concern and decided to see if they could change his behavior by withdrawing their attention from his inappropriate behaviors and give attention when he responded appropriately. It worked.

5. Ben learned to go to the dining room by himself to

    get _____ and _____.

---

5. food
   attention

Ben, of course, was being watched very closely. The staff had no intention of letting him suffer from malnutrition. They felt that he was well enough fed and healthy enough to miss a few meals. If this could possibly result in his giving up his withdrawing behavior, it would be well worth the inconvenience to Ben.

A Study in Correcting Dressing Behavior

Delores began to wear excessive amounts of clothing. She would put on several sweaters, shawls, dresses, under garments and stockings. At times, she would wear as many as two dozen pairs of stockings. She also wrapped sheets and towels around her body and wrapped towels around her head in turban-like fashion. Generally the clothes she wore weighed almost twenty-five pounds. She was certainly one of the most bizarre looking patients in the ward.

In order to get this patient to decrease this behavior of over-dressing, it was decided that she would not be permitted to enter the dining room unless she weighed a certain amount. Each day this prescribed amount was reduced a pound or two so that when she arrived at the dining room, she could not enter unless she removed some of her clothing. If she refused to remove her clothing to meet the prescribed weight, she simply missed that meal.

6. The behavior they wanted to _____

    in frequency was "adding clothes beyond that

    needed to be appropriately dressed."

At first the patient missed a few meals. She also threw some tantrums, shouting, crying, throwing chairs. These inappropriate behaviors were ignored and they disappeared. Soon, however, she was readily discarding the necessary amount of clothing to meet the weight requirements. In a few weeks, the patient was appearing at the dining room wearing a dress, under garments, a pair of stockings and a pair of shoes —indistinguishable in her dress from all the other patients.

7. The reward which was used to get this change in

    Delores was _____.

---

6. decrease

7. food

A secondary result of this change in her dressing behavior was also a change in her participation in social affairs This behavior increased. Previously she had spent most of her time secluded in her room. About this time, her family came to visit her and they insisted on taking her home for a visit. This was the first time in nine years her parents took her out of the hospital. They hadn't wanted to take her home before because her manner of dressing made her look like a "circus freak."

 8. There is considerable hope that her new be-

havior will be continued due to this extra

_____ from her family.

The adult in an institution is subject to change much as our children might be. In an institution, the resident looks to the staff and a limited environment to supply his needs. This is especially true of long term residents and can probably account for some of the truly amazing changes which have been brought about under such conditions. However, as was noted in the chapter on adolescence, as the individual moves out into a more complex and relatively uncontrolled environment, our changing him becomes a far more complicated task. We can look upon our potential for changing a given individual as a factor of (1) what do we have for him and (2) how much does he want it. Therefore it becomes necessary to obtain the cooperation and help of other persons significant in the life of the person—especially the person himself.

Training Self-Control

The otherwise independent adult with a problem comes under our influence only insofar as we control his sources of satisfaction. However, an understanding of behavior principles and how to use them can be employed by the troubled adult to bring about changes in himself. Such behavior change implemented by ourselves can be labeled self-control and can be engineered to a large extent by the individual most concerned. Much research needs to be done in the area of self-control of annoying or disturbing behaviors. Work in this area is merely beginning. The attention of other people (social rewards) is very important for changing our behavior patterns. There is not much reward in struggling (often times painfully) to get rid of old, undesirable habits and develop new ones if there is no one to recognize our efforts and success. Behavior we find distressing to ourselves may really be distressing because of other people's response to it.

---

8. attention

9. Self-control is most effectively carried out when

——————————————————————— are

correctly employed.

Obtaining Environmental Feedback

The overweight woman may not get concerned about her over-weight until she thinks her husband is displeased with her figure, men in general are not giving her a second glance, or her friends make snide remarks about her waist line or dress size. We call this environmental "feedback" and it can be picked up from a mirror or a scale as well. In this age, our society has put much emphasis on the slim look. We are beseiged every day by magazine and television ads that portray the slender person as healthy, wholesome and attractive. In the previous century, skinny people were frowned upon and people with "meat on their bones" were considered healthy and desirable. In other countries of the world this is still very much the case. But because of this expectation in our society, people have become very self-conscious about their figures. Much money, time and effort is spent either in reducing the frequency of their eating behavior, or increasing the frequency of those behaviors (exercising) that use up calories. Here again, it is the attention of other people or environmental feedback that controls our behavior.

10. What others tell us about ourselves by word or

deed serves as environmental ————————

and helps us to know ourselves.

A Plan for Losing Weight

Organizations have sprung up to give individuals the social support they need to decrease the frequency of their eating behavior. These organizations make maximum use of the principles outlined in this manual. Meetings are held once a week where public rewards and punishments are doled out for having lost or not lost the prescribed amount. Large losses receive much attention and praise. Those who failed to lose (or, heaven forbid, gained) are severely ridiculed in front of everyone.

———————————————————————————————————

9. behavioral principles   10. feedback

The following outline will serve as an example of engineering which might be applied by an overweight person. It can be seen that whoever makes use of such a design needs to make a rather detailed study of his individual problem in order to bring it under conrol.

11. The use of recording charts provides

_____ feedback which

can be most useful in control of behavior.

LOSING WEIGHT AND MAINTAINING THE DESIRED WEIGHT

1. First, and most important—keep an accurate daily record of your weight. (Be sure to use the same scale, at the same time each day. Find a professional balance scale which will read accurately to the ¼ lb.)
2. Analyze your eating habits—circumstances surrounding your *extra* food intake, *when* you eat, where, and so on.
3. Establish *environmental* controls:
   a. Eat in a certain place—not all over the house or in your work area.
   b. Eliminate all food from your immediate environment which can be eaten without careful preparation, i.e., snacks, etc.
   c. Always sit down to a carefully set place at the table and eat only one helping of the foods planned for.
   d. Prepare only enough for one meal at a time. (Eliminate picking up and eating left-overs.)
   e. Refer to your analysis of your eating habits (2). If you eat between meals or after supper, engage in an activity which cannot be carried on while eating—at times when you feel "hungry." (Smoking, gardening, etc.)
4. Establish *self* controls:
   a. Eat slowly. Put down utensils after every mouthful.
   b. Partway through the meal—stop and sit relaxed, without eating for two or three minutes.
   c. Avoid becoming really deprived of food (starving yourself). Count on losing an average of one to two pounds per week at most.
   d. Eat a carefully balanced diet so that there is no deprivation for a particular needed food element. (Deprivation can upset self-control.)
   e. Reward yourself through self-approval; a book or a movie for reaching weekly goals. Set up long-term rewards such as new clothes or vacation days.
5. Establish *social* controls:
   a. Get the interest and support of a significant person. Put your weight record where this person can see it and reward you for your progress.
   b. If possible, involve a group of persons in the weight loss program, keeping track of each other's records, sharing problems and establishing rewards.

---

11. environmental

The following account is how an underweight individual used behavioral principles to put on weight by increasing the frequency of her eating behavior. Sharon weighed 87 pounds and wanted to weigh at least 100 pounds if not more but had never been able to get over 90 pounds except when she was carrying a child. She had studied scientific principles of behavior change in a psychology class and sought advice for setting up a program to increase her eating behavior thereby hoping to increase her weight. She had made. attempts to increase her eating habits before but had not been able to break the 90 pound barrier. Her husband agreed to assist in any way and to provide the rewards necessary to support any behavior directed toward this goal.

Sharon smoked approximately a pack of cigarettes a day. The approach she had attempted earlier was to cut out all smoking behavior as she believed smoking reduced her appetite. This was probably why her earlier attempts failed. The pleasure and reward of smoking was too strong for her to find an increase in eating behavior an adequate replacement. It was decided instead that she should continue smoking but that she had to eat 200 calories of food before smoking a cigarette. In this way the cigarette could serve as a reward for the behavior of eating 200 calories of food.

12. The immediate reward for eating was
_____. This was necessary to
make eating a more _____
event.

Starting with a pack of cigarettes at the beginning of each day, whenever she wanted to smoke she first was to eat an amount of food that supplied 200 calories or more. This was to be recorded. At the end of the day, she would turn this list and her remaining cigarettes (if there were any) over to her husband who responded positively to her progress. In addition, her husband agreed to pay her three dollars for every pound of weight she gained over her baseline of 87 pounds. This had been established as her average weight for a one week period.

Sharon weighed herself each morning before breakfast and kept a chart posted on her bathroom wall to record her progress (see Figure 3). The chart provided environmental feedback. It was only a matter of days before she passed the 90 pound mark and was making rapid

12. smoking
    desirable (pleasant)

progress toward her 100 pound goal. She was gaining approximately
a pound a week. Sharon had also been experiencing frequent stomach
upsets, discomfort and subsequent loss of appetite. As her weight increased, this distress occurred less and less often.

FIGURE 3. SHARON'S PROGRESS IN GAINING WEIGHT

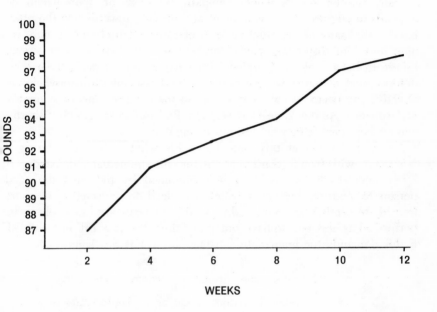

Other Problems

The use of behavioral principles are being explored in the treatment
of alcoholism, smoking behavior, and other undesirable habits. One
of the difficulties in treating these conditions is that immediate results
of drinking alcohol, smoking cigarettes, etc., are so powerful or pleasur-
able to the person that it is difficult to get him to stop this behavior or
reduce it to where it no longer threatens his health or causes personal or
family distress. The elimination of unusual or extreme fears called
"phobias" are also being treated with behavior laws. The techniques
used in treating these problems are more complex than the simple use of
rewards to increase appropriate behavior but nonetheless the approaches are based on behavioral laws. (For more information on these
more sophisticated approaches consult reference six at the end of this
chapter.)

Use of behavioral laws for maintaining appropriate behaviors in the aged individual is essentially an extension of their use in adult life with two general exceptions. The aged individual is one who is becoming dependent on a more and more limited environment. It is now actually simpler for us whose company he seeks or upon whom he depends to engineer his environment and provide rewards. On the other hand, with many of his usual avenues of satisfaction closing to him, we may find him displaying panic, anxiety, mental depression or simply failure to behave at all. Coupled with what may be a perfectly natural deterioration of aging we are struck with the seemingly overwhelming negative prospects and often give way to mere expressions of sympathy and concern. At the same time we may find our visits growing shorter and farther apart as they are less rewarding to us.

It is important at this point to decide what is best for the aged tempered with some consideration for his immediate demands. A lively interest in life may best be maintained by requiring the aged person to perform behaviors which will lead to satisfaction of more immediate needs. Behaviors leading to distant goals are less likely to be performed as he seems to have run out of time. We may call him childish in his demands for immediate satisfactions, yet it has some logic.

13. Satisfaction given or acquired for appropriate behaviors in the aged should relate to _____ rather than _____ goals.

If we recall the work with the long term hospitalized patient, we note that when they found they could reliably get some of the things they wanted through specified behaviors, not only were the behaviors rapidly increased but there was a general increase in other interests and behaviors. This was usually accompanied by expressions of renewed interest in life and increased socialization. The same general framework will often get similar results with the aged.

A Problem with Grandmother

Martin found that his much loved grandmother was beginning to annoy him. His visits were decreasing in frequency and he often went

---

13. immediate
    distant

way irritated by her increasing complaining and deepening negative 123 iews of life. Regretting very much this unfortunate change in their re- itionship he discussed the situation with a friend trained in behavioral rocedures. He was advised to follow a prescribed plan. His first move ras to schedule a series of ten visits of thirty minutes each during ie next two months. During these visits he was to keep a record of ie amount of time she spent on unpleasant topics which she frequently rought up. He kept a stop watch in his hand inside a pocket and pressed ie starter whenever she introduced an unpleasant topic and kept it epressed until she mentioned a more pleasant subject or stopped speak- ig. This gave Martin a fairly accurate baseline of the time she spent in etailing physical complaints, reports of local crimes or attacks against articular political situations. He attempted to keep his own responses s nearly usual as possible. When five of the periods had ended, he raphed the results as follows:

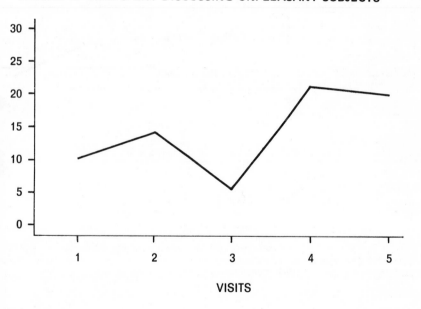

FIGURE 4. TIME SPENT DISCUSSING UNPLEASANT SUBJECTS

VISITS

14. The data in this graph represents the _____ frequency of Grandma's talking about subjects Martin didn't want to hear.

4. baseline

124   During the next five periods, he responded with interest only to neutral or pleasant topics, ignoring or walking away when the unpleasant subjects were introduced. At the same time he kept track of the time again in the same way. Here are the results of the second five weeks.

FIGURE 4. CONT.

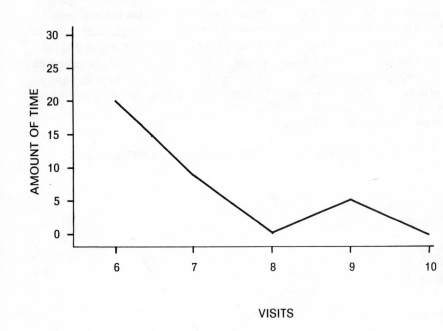

VISITS

15. Martin used _____ or _____ as a response for decreasing Grandma's talk on subjects he didn't care to listen to.

A dramatic change and it persisted! He was delighted with this change in her "personality."

In discussing her one day with another relative, however, he was disappointed to hear Sue complain that Grandma whines constantly and is certainly not her old pleasant self. He decided to show her his charts and explained his plan. After a short time using the same system of

---

15. ignoring   walking away

ignoring and responding, she too experienced a profound change in Grandma's "personality." Now others too began to notice how much more cheerful she had become. Not knowing Sue's and Martin's secret, they speculated that her health had improved or that she was responding to a new vitamin!

Keeping the Aged Physically Active

Another area of concern is keeping the aged physically active so that they get a minimum amount of exercise. Once the elderly person stops moving, invalidism sets in very quickly. Many elderly persons find even a minimum amount of physical exertion an inconvenience. They would rather spend most of the day sitting and smoking, playing cards, looking through magazines, talking or just looking off into space.

16. It is obvious by now that if we want elderly persons to increase the amount of time they exercise, we should ———————————— them for it.

The elderly men of one nursing home spent much of their day in such pursuits. The attendant on duty felt they needed to move about more and get some mild exercise. Whenever she found a male patient sitting idly about, she would flirtatiously attempt to bribe or coax him in exercising. If any of these men responded to her persuasions and got up to exercise, she felt well rewarded for her efforts and set off looking for someone else to keep active, alert and fit. We, by now, realize immediately that this attentive young lady had the pay-off just reversed. The men were receiving social attention for being coaxed into doing exercise. But once they started to perform the actual exercising behavior, they lost her attention. Consistent with behavior principles, we can be certain that these elderly gentlemen spent more time being coaxed than exercising. The attractive female attendant was informed of her misuse of behavioral principles and told to do just the opposite of what she had been doing. Rewarding the gentlemen with attention, fuss over them when exercising and ignore them if they were merely sitting. The desired results followed quickly. She, in fact, had to be cautioned to go a little easy. There was fear that one of the men might suffer a heart attack due to over-exertion!

16. reward

As indicated in the first chapter of this manual, the prospects for the future in eliminating "problems in living" are indeed exciting. Just as awareness and application of physical laws are permitting us to transform the material quality of our lives so, hopefully, will awareness and application of behavioral laws permit us to transform the behavioral qualities or character of man.

As with all scientific knowledge, it can be used wisely for the betterment of life or it can be subverted to the whims of those who desire to exploit and misuse. But this too is a matter of learning or training and man can be taught to "behave" for the betterment of life rather than to exploit it. Through use of behavioral laws "cooperative behaviors" among men can be strengthened and increased and exploitive behaviors decreased.

Man may be on the threshold of a "behavioral revolution" of the same magnitude as that of the Industrial Revolution! Let us hope that it does not succumb to some of the initial abuses.

This case history was taken from: Patterson, Gerald; Ray, Roberta; Shaw, David; "Direct Intervention in Families of Deviant Children"; *Oregon Research Institute;* Vol. 8; No. 9; December, 1968 (Slight changes or modifications have been made in the text of this case history so that it would be easily understandable to the audience to whom this manual is directed, persons with no previous background in scientific behavior theory.)

Harold was eight years old. "He was reported to be very active, dangerously aggressive, and not achieving in school. He was deemed sufficiently disruptive" in the classroom that school officials planned to expel "him from school if some dramatic changes in his behavior did not begin to occur."

"The parents viewed Harold as a quiet, stubborn sort of social isolate who was rarely a serious behavior problem at home. While the mother was somewhat concerned about the difficulties in school," the father "dismissed the importance of the school problem with the comment that neither he nor his other sons had done particularly well in school. In fact, he seemed rather pleased. . .at his sons's aggressive behaviors. He did, however, agree to. . .participation in a treatment program if it would insure that Harold would not be expelled from school."

"Harold was the fifth of six children, having four brothers and one older sister. The older boys in the family had also been conduct and behavior problems in school. The family lived on a small farm in a semi-rural area. The father was a part-time farmer and construction worker. The mother worked part-time as a nurse's aide in a rest home."

"Baseline observation in the home tended to support the parents' report of very low frequencies of inappropriate behavior for all of the children. However, baseline observation in the classroom showed high frequencies of such behaviors as inappropriate noise and talking, nonattending, movement around the classroom and physical aggression. Observation during recess indicated that Harold spent about half of this time either engaged in aggressive behavior or in solitary play; the remaining half was spent in group activities. Though Harold was in a third grade class he performed at the first grade level; he could read only a few words and do only very simple arithmetic problems. He had difficulty recognizing the letters of the alphabet or numbers of two digits or more. His only interest in school seemed to be in drawing, for which he showed some skill."

The plans for a three stage treatment program included attempts to: "1) increase the rate of Harold's attending behaviors, 2) increase his school skills, 3) reduce the frequency of aggressive-isolate behaviors."

Stage one began "by explaining to Harold and the class that he would be helped to learn to sit still and concentrate by a 'magic work box.' They were told that this box would keep a count of points earned by Harold for attending to his school work and that at the end of the class the points could be exchanged for candies which Harold would then share with the entire class. Harold was told that this 'magic work box' (a simple buzzer and counter activated by a remote control switch) would add up points only if he attended to the work assigned to him." He was started with copying numbers and drawing (a task which he already showed interest in).

"Harold eagerly entered into the 'game' and during the first session earned many candies and the spontaneous applause of his classmates when his total points were announced. During six days of sessions of twenty minutes each, the amount of time Harold had to spend attending to the task before receiving a point was increased from ten seconds to thirty seconds. As his attention span began to increase and he became more successful in performing the task (and earning more points for himself and his classmates) his social relations with his classmates also changed. His aggressive behaviors dropped to nearly a zero rate and the amount of social interaction increased. Because of these spontaneous changes, there was no need to set up a program to change his aggressive-isolate behavior" (step 3 in the program).

"The planning for stage two of developing competence in basic school skills was undertaken with the involvement of his teacher. She was encouraged by Harold's changed behavior and assisted in developing arithmetic assignments where each problem was assigned a number of possible points based on the difficulty level. An above average student, whom Harold had chosen on several occasions to help distribute the candy rewards, was selected as a coach. He was given the answers to the problems and a counter for recording the points Harold earned. The student coach and Harold worked together for thirty minutes each day for one week. The coach was to oversee the completion of each problem. When a problem was completed he rewarded Harold with a smile and said, 'good.' If the answer was correct he also recorded a point on the counter. Incorrect problems were repeated, with help from the coach if necessary, until arold arrived at the correct answer. Points were adjusted downward if more han one attempt was necessary to get the answer. At the end of each day's ssion, the total number of points Harold had earned were announced to the ass; in addition Harold colored in the appropriate amount of space on a 'point nermometer' drawn on the blackboard. A special candy reward was promised if ne points 'went over the top' of the thermometer at the end of the week." arold successfully earned this reward at the end of the week and received dditional support from his classmates when he shared this candy reward with nem.

At this point the control of the program and dispensing of rewards was urned over to the parents and the teacher. The teacher was trained in the dis-ensing of token rewards for school work and for appropriate rather than appropriate classroom behaviors. "Two cards were taped to Harold's desk. On ne card the teacher marked each fifteen minute time interval during which arold did *not* engage in disruptive behavior but did attend to his assigned work. certain number of marks could then be traded in for a 'free-time period' uring which Harold could paint, listen to music or investigate science exhibits : the back of the room. The teacher found this system so uncomplicated and fective in the control of behavior that she soon had every child in the class on ich a system and all were diligently working for 'free-time' points."

"On the second card the teacher recorded points earned for completing ssignments; a copy of this card was taken home each night and a total number f points was recorded by the mother. Harold's father agreed that when a pecified number was reached, Harold and his father would go on a fishing trip."

"Harold was allowed to earn extra points for the fishing trip by explaining is daily school work to his parents after dinner. This was a difficult task since ich topics had not been a part of the family's after-dinner conversation. A brief aining session was conducted to show the parents how to proceed."

"Six months after the start of this program, Harold's inappropriate ehaviors were occurring at the same or a lower rate than those of his classmates ee Figure 5). At recess Harold was now spending approximately 99% of his me interacting with other children on the playground. The hitting, shoving, and reatening behavior toward the other children had all but disappeared (see igure 6).

Harold had learned a set of behaviors which served to reliably produce social ewards in the classroom. These behaviors now took the place of the appropriate behaviors such as hitting, making noise or moving about the assroom which had been his primary means of producing social consequences the past.

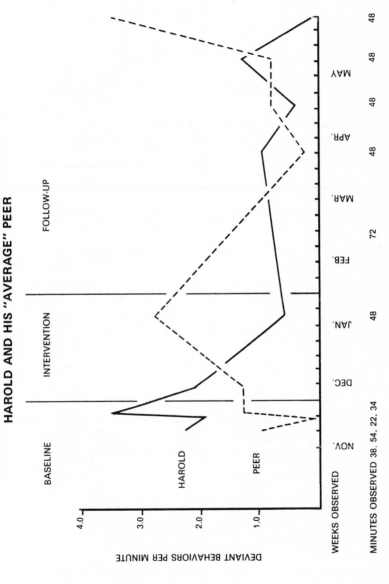

FIGURE 5. RATE OF DEVIANT BEHAVIOR IN THE CLASSROOM HAROLD AND HIS "AVERAGE" PEER

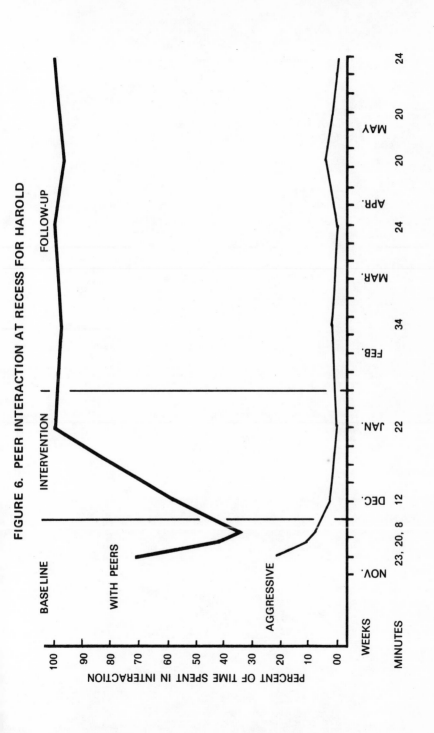

FIGURE 6. PEER INTERACTION AT RECESS FOR HAROLD

or those readers who are interested in the ideas and principles pre-
nted in this manual and who would like to follow through with some
ore study and reading in this area, the authors provide the following
st of books.

Living with Children, Patterson and Gullion; Research Press, Champaign, Illinois, 1968. A very practical, elementary book for parents. It is even more basic and easier to understand than this manual and would be a good follow-up reading for those parents who want to get the laws of behavior down pat. It is written in "teaching machine" format.

Behavioral Therapy, Shaeffer and Martin; McGraw Hill, New York, 1969. A general overall approach to the same material presented in this manual but at a slightly more technical level. Specific programs for handling many kinds of behavior problems are presented. Highly recommended as the next book you read if you want to continue investigating this area.

How to Use Contingency Contracting in the Classroom, Homme; Research Press, Champaign, Illinois, 1969. Ideas and techniques for teachers who wish to capitalize on behavioral laws in structuring the total classroom environment.

The Token Economy. Ayllon and Azrin; Appleton-Century-Crofts, N.Y., 1968. A manual based on the work done by these two authors at a state mental institution. It documents the effectiveness of behavior laws in correcting the inappropriate behavior patterns of the "mentally ill." The patients had previously spent many years of their lives in the hospital and been given up as hopelessly incurable.

Teaching the Mentally Retarded—A Handbook for Ward Personnel, Bensberg; Southern Regional Education Board, Atlanta, Georgia, 1967. A very basic manual for persons working with the mentally retarded. It has many illustrations to show just how one proceeds through the various training programs for dressing, feeding, etc. Easy to understand format.

A Psychological Approach to Abnormal Behavior, Ullman and Krasner; Prentice Hall, Englewood Cliffs, New Jersey, 1969. A textbook for college level psychology courses in abnormal behavior. The whole range of "abnormal" behavior is covered and discussed in terms of behavioral principles.